FATHER HUNGER

◆

Fathers,
Daughters
& Food

◆

Margo Maine, Ph.D.

Preface by Craig Johnson, Ph.D.

SIMON & SCHUSTER

LONDON·SYDNEY·NEW YORK·TOKYO·SINGAPORE·TORONTO

First published in Great Britain by
Simon & Schuster Ltd in 1993
A Paramount Communications Company

Simon & Schuster Ltd
West Garden Place
Kendal Street
London W2 2AQ

Simon & Schuster of Australia Pty Ltd
Sydney

A CIP catalogue record for this book is
available from the British Library
ISBN 0-671-71288-8

Printed and bound in Great Britain by
Butler & Tanner Ltd, Frome

NOTE:

The author and publisher of this book intend for this publication to provide accurate information. It is sold with the understanding that it is meant to complement, not substitute for, professional medical and/or psychological services.

TABLE OF CONTENTS

Acknowledgements   v

Preface by Craig Johnson, Ph.D.   vii

Introduction   xi

Part One: The Origins of Father Hunger

1. Father Hunger and the Pursuit of Thinness   3

2. Ten Myths About Fathers, Daughters and Food   13

3. Fathers as Second-Class Citizens   26

4. A Shaky Foundation for Fatherhood: 42
    Male Psychological Development

5. The Daughter's Dilemma: 56
    Female Psychological Development

Part Two: The Experience of Father Hunger

6. Damage to a Daughter's Emotions and Identity   73

7. Conflicts Surrounding Sexuality, Body Image,   94
    and Food

8. The Family's Functional Dysfunction   110

9. The Legacy of Loyalty   129

Part Three: The Solutions to Father Hunger

10. How Men can Overcome Father Hunger   149
11. How Mothers can Help   179
12. How Daughters can Survive Father Hunger   204
13. Why We All Must Prevent Father Hunger   224

Appendices

Appendix A: Suggested Strategies for Educators   227
Appendix B: Suggested Strategies for Physicians   233
Appendix C: Suggested Strategies for Therapists   237
Appendix D: Suggested Strategies for Other   240
             Professionals and Adults
Notes   243
Index   251

ACKNOWLEDGMENTS

I am one of the fortunate few who escaped the experience of father hunger. My dad was available, affirming, and affectionate. He invited me into his world, but shared equally in mine and in the family's life. My mother always supported and encouraged his involvement. I thank them both and dedicate this book to my father's memory.

I also thank my husband for his endless patience and understanding when this project took precedence over our daily lives. His constant support has been essential to my accomplishing this goal. I also appreciated the validation provided by my family, friends, and colleagues, and their tolerance and forgiveness when I was preoccupied or unavailable.

The support provided by Marianna Nelson, Research Coordinator at Newington Children's Hospital, has been priceless throughout this process. Her editing, word-processing, and understanding of the concepts I hoped to communicate in *Father Hunger* were invaluable. I could not have completed it without her help, guidance, and intuition as a writer.

The opportunity to work with Gürze Books has also been a great gift. I deeply appreciate the conceptual contributions and endless editing provided by Lindsey Hall and Leigh Cohn. I thank them for their commitment to educating the public about eating disorders and their persistence and encouragement as my raw notions about father hunger gradually evolved into a meaningful and comprehensible theory.

Finally, I thank the young women and their families who have let me into their lives and taught me so much. I hope this book enhances your healing.

◆ ◆ ◆

PREFACE
by Craig Johnson, Ph.D.

The question of why people would engage in a variety of life-threatening behaviors, such as self-starvation or purging in order to achieve thinness, has challenged clinicians for over two centuries. Theories of etiology have ranged from demonic possession to neuro-chemical imbalances. The increase in the incidence of anorexia nervosa and bulimia over the last two decades has provoked a flurry of research regarding the causes of these disorders. The results have refined our understanding of why some individuals become obsessively preoccupied with food, weight and their bodies.

This research indicates that there are striking demographic similarities within the group. Nine out of ten are female and in ninety percent of the cases, the onset occurs between the ages of 15 and 30. Overall, those most affected are single, Caucasian, college-educated females from middle- to upper-class intact families. It is important to note that the prevalence of anorexia nervosa and bulimia is directly related to the degree of westernization in different countries. For example, they are as common in Tokyo as in the United States, but they are virtually nonexistent in rural Japan where there is little westernization. Also, the fact that these disorders hardly exist in the lower socioeconomic groups suggests that they are highly affected by sociocultural factors, and that essentially they are culture-bound syndromes.

Several authors, including Dr. Maine, have speculated about recent changes that have occurred in western culture that might account for the increase in eating disorders and weight preoccupation, particularly among young women. More specifically, the argument is made that beginning in the mid-1960s "thinness" became a highly idealized look. In an effort to achieve this look, many young women engaged in a variety of weight-loss behaviors including severe calorie restriction, extreme exercise and purging behaviors, such as self-induced vomiting, laxative or diuretic abuse. For some, this pursuit deteriorated into a psychiatric disorder. While the sociocultural theory is extremely useful in explaining why we would have seen such a rapid increase in anorexia and bulimia, it does not explain why only some young women, about two out of one hundred, become more clinically impaired than others.

The question of why some young women would develop an extreme eating disorder given the same cultural climate remains elusive. More biologically-oriented theorists are attempting to demonstrate that prolonged calorie restrictions, sustained low body weight or repeated bingeing and vomiting creates biological changes that continue to drive many of the symptoms. More psychologically-oriented theorists hypothesize that the group who is most at risk for developing problems with food and body-image have experienced significant disappointment in relationships with people closest to them. In response to this disappointment, they begin to rely on things such as food, drugs, or alcohol to try to meet their needs.

The emphasis on "relationship disappointment" is where Dr. Maine focuses her work. Previous explorations of this issue have concentrated almost exclusively on difficulties in the mother and child relationship. This has had the unfortunate effect of making many mothers feel that they were solely responsible for their daughters' problems. Refreshingly, this author has shifted the lens to focus on the importance of the fathers' role in the emotional development of their daughters.

Dr. Maine coins the phrase "father hunger" to describe the natural longing that children have for their fathers, which, when unfulfilled, can lead to a variety of problems. She examines how multigenerational and sociocultural factors have resulted in fathers becoming not only physically, but emotionally disconnected from their families, and how this distance affects the development of sexuality, body-image, self-esteem, and identity in adolescent daughters.

Throughout the book, Dr. Maine translates sophisticated and difficult psychological theories into a language that is understandable to the lay reader. She avoids "father bashing" by offering an evenhanded explanation of the differences in psychological development between men and women which causes men to have difficulty with emotional expression and nurturing skills.

She offers specific recommendations for how to repair the father/daughter relationship. She speaks to fathers directly, conveying what changes they need to make, as well as what mothers can do to facilitate these changes. Finally, she encourages daughters to risk improving relationships with their fathers as part of their recovery process. Dr. Maine offers solid advice that is challenging and accessible to all family members.

I believe the success of a book is often determined by it appearing at the right time with the right information. Unquestionably, the time is right for a book that focuses on the importance of fathers in their daughters' lives. Since fathers should represent one-half of our experience with primary caretakers and should be at least one of the most important men in a woman's life, it is frightening that books like this are just starting to appear.

This book also has the right information. Dr. Maine has done a masterful job of integrating sociocultural events, developmental data, and systems theory into a comprehensive and readable explanation of how impaired father/daughter relationships might heighten the likelihood of a young woman developing problems with food. I found this book useful, and I am confident it will be helpful to patients, their families and professionals.

Craig Johnson, Ph.D. authored *The Etiology and Treatment of Bulimia Nervosa* and *Psychodynamic Treatment of Anorexia Nervosa and Bulimia*. He is one of the world's foremost authorities on eating disorders.

♦ ♦ ♦

INTRODUCTION

Soon after I began to treat young people with eating disorders in 1980, I decided to specialize in this area. I felt challenged as well as baffled by the complex interactions between mind, body, and soul, and I knew I had much to learn if I were to be an effective therapist for these individuals. Many of my mentors and colleagues warned me about limiting the scope of my practice so early in my career. They believed that eating disorders were a fad that would last only a few years. In contrast, I strongly sensed that we would be seeing more and more people with problems surrounding food and body-image because of unrealistic and negative cultural dictates about beauty, perfection, dieting, and emotional expression. Unfortunately, I was right. By 1983, we had seen so many children and adolescents with eating disorders at the hospital where I worked, that we developed a formal interdisciplinary program to provide inpatient and outpatient services, individualized to meet the needs of the patients and their families.

My clinical work has introduced me to thousands of people whose lives have been affected by problems with food, such as anorexia nervosa, bulimia, compulsive eating, yo-yo dieting, poor body-image, and weight-preoccupation. These people are from different socioeconomic and cultural backgrounds with diverse family histories; they range in age from infants to grandparents, and the severity of illness varies from mild to severe. I have seen xii ◆ FATHER HUNGER

how girls commonly grow up hating their bodies and expressing this and other pain through food. Undereating, dieting, overeating, compulsive eating, exercise abuse, eating disorders, and the health problems associated with malnutrition are frequent results, as are difficulties with intimacy, relationships, and self-esteem. We need to reverse these trends soon. Too many people are suffering.

Probably the most important lesson from my experience has been to listen to my patients, for they hold the solutions to their problems. By listening carefully, I have further discovered that the development of and recovery from eating problems does not just concern women or mother-daughter relationships, as much of the literature indicates. Fathers play a crucial role.

I'd like to share how I discovered this fact. When I first became involved in this field, I would spend a couple of hours in the evening reading the clinical literature and latest research. I felt I was learning a lot, until one day I had an experience that was so powerful it completely re-shaped my thinking as a therapist.

I was sitting with a 15-year-old patient in her room. Barbara had just been admitted and I was seeing her for the first time. She had been in outpatient treatment for anorexia for a year and had recently developed bulimic symptoms as well. She was a beautiful, shy, emaciated girl. I asked her a few questions and she gradually began to talk about herself, her family, her feelings of hopelessness, and her parents' marriage. When Barbara told me how she felt about her father, I suddenly understood that I was interpreting what she was telling me in terms of the theories I had read the night before! This was a powerful, intuitive moment for me and it became a turning point in my career as a therapist. I realized that I could help her more if I stopped sifting what she said through a theoretical framework. This meant that I had to stop trying to be like and think like all the theorists I had been reading and that I would have to have total confidence in my ability to help patients like Barbara and in their ability to help themselves.

Coincidentally, Barbara had been talking about her father when this revelation came to me. Most of the material I had read was about mothers. Little importance was placed on the role of fathers in either the causes or the treatment of eating disorders. This imbalance bothered me because of the role my own father played in my life. My development as a professional who could help others was strongly tied to our very close relationship, through which I felt my father's influence, values, love, and respect for me. As Barbara spoke, vivid images of my own father swept into my mind.

I wondered what my life would have been like if I had had a different kind of father. It was hard to picture growing up without his support and interest, his constant validation of my self-worth, and his desire to spend time with me. I remembered all the letters he wrote to me during that homesick first semester of college. Other memories surfaced, and I immediately understood how divergent Barbara's experience and mine were, because we had such different dads.

All of a sudden, I felt I was in uncharted territory. My personal experience was in sharp contrast to this young woman's. I had never felt deprived of my father's love and therefore I didn't hunger for him the way she did for her father. Turning to the clinical literature didn't help. Barbara's description of her dad did not match the theories about fathers of eating disordered daughters. He was not uninterested or uncaring, as fathers were typically depicted. Instead, he was very concerned about his family, but inept as a parent. When I met him I observed a man who would do anything to help his daughter recover; yet he didn't have a clue as to what she needed from him. He only knew how to buy her things, hoping that she would be happy again. He didn't know how to give of himself because he had never been shown how. Lucky for Barbara, he was willing to learn. Through family therapy, he became more emotionally expressive and more actively involved in Barbara's life. The changes he made helped her to recover.

Years later, I still think about Barbara and that first hour of therapy when she described her hunger for an emotional connection with her dad. She thought that having a different body would please him, so she dieted, lost weight, over-exercised, and purged, masking her pain and emptiness.

Treating Barbara and other people with eating problems has sensitized me to how much girls need their dads to help them develop into young women who feel positive, strong, assertive, confident of themselves, and able to negotiate relationships. When dads are uninvolved, absent, or inconsistent, their daughters experience what Barbara was describing—a deep unrelenting father hunger.

Over the years I have discovered that father hunger is not restricted to female adolescents, nor is its expression limited to eating disorders. Both boys and girls grow up with this yearning for dad, but until recently we have not explored it. Because of the cultural roles we have ascribed to men and women, father hunger is now a nearly universal experience in western societies, expressed in many self-destructive behaviors.

It is time to focus on the positive and crucial role that fathers can play in their daughters' emerging identity and self-esteem. There is no substitute for a father's love. Similarly, there may be nothing worse than being deprived of or feeling uncertain about it.

The first section of this book examines the origins of father hunger. It demonstrates how our culture has influenced family functioning by perpetuating myths that convey minimal importance to the father's role in the family, particularly in raising daughters. This section also clarifies the dilemmas young women face as they struggle to meet uncertain and conflicting expectations, subsequent to the rapid changes in sex roles during the latter half of the 20th century.

The second section describes how father hunger can become so devastating that young women wage war with their bodies to cope with the inner emptiness. It further illustrates how a limited paternal presence creates a loss for the whole family. Case presentations and vignettes are utilized to convey how father hunger feels.

The final section conceptualizes how we can change our roles and myths so that men and women can share power and responsibility more equitably, and thus work together more effectively both in the family and in the world. Separate chapters address fathers, mothers, and daughters. The last chapter explores what we can all do to create a more positive role for fathers and to prevent the eating problems and body-image dissatisfaction that plague so many young people. The appendices include specific suggestions for various professionals who have influence in the lives of young people and their families.

I have tried to stimulate readers to think about their relationships with their fathers. You may discover some old scars or open wounds in the process. Pay attention to these, as they are opportunities for healing. When you finish reading this book, I hope you can find ways to create better relationships between men and women and between fathers and families. Imagine children feeling loved and secure in their relationships with their dads. Imagine men feeling comfortable and free to express emotions, nurture children, need others, and spend more time and energy with their families. Imagine fathers being more than family providers and protectors. Imagine men and women sharing power and responsibility both at home and at work. Imagine an end to father hunger.

PART ONE

THE ORIGINS OF FATHER HUNGER

CHAPTER 1

◆ ◆ ◆

FATHER HUNGER AND THE PURSUIT OF THINNESS

Father hunger is a deep, persistent desire for emotional connection with the father that is experienced by all children. When this normal craving is satisfied, children are likely to grow up feeling confident, secure, strong, and "good enough." Often, however, this yearning is not acknowledged and the child's hunger and need for a bond with father grows. This causes self-doubt, pain, anxiety, and depression, as well as learning and behavior problems. For our purposes, father hunger will refer to this unfulfilled longing for father, which for girls and women, often translates into conflicts about food and weight.

Adults may continue to suffer this hunger if they have not found a way to relate to their fathers or resolve their feelings of loss. They bring this longing to new relationships as spouses and parents, and in this way, father hunger is passed on. Although rarely identified, discussed, or confronted, it becomes a shared, multi-generational experience that we unfortunately accept as a normal and natural by-product of western culture. Thus, our society is organized around assumptions and practices that allow most children to grow up not really knowing their fathers.

We have adapted to our father hunger despite the suffering it causes. The accepted social roles for men and women—the family structure itself—have evolved to support this condition rather than to challenge it. Cultural dictates and myths have limited men's roles, suggesting that mothers are important but fathers are expendable. Ultimately, this has created a loss for all family members. Children must be satisfied with a minimal relationship with their fathers, mothers have to do most of the day-to-day parenting, and men feel inept and incapable in their roles at home.

The cycle of father hunger is handed down from one generation to the next. The way we treat men and the expectations we have of them are the primary contributors to this pattern. From early in their development, males are forced to be separate, isolated, and unemotional. They are encouraged to achieve but not to feel. Consequently, when they become parents, fathering requires more intimacy than most men can handle. Thus, each generation enters adulthood hungry for a connection with father but lacking awareness of the dysfunctional pattern or the skills to break it.

Father hunger is a special problem for daughters because they are taught from infancy to put relationships first. Since they value close connections, they find their father's distance very unsettling. They crave contact with their dads but are confused by this desire. More and more young women are coping with this conflict by dieting and obsessing about their weight, in order to conform to cultural standards, and thereby get their father's approval.

This book explores how father hunger affects both adult men and adolescent daughters and how it leads to "If only I were skinny" reasoning and the rejection of physical and psychological needs of women who are obsessed with food and body image. Hopefully, recognition of these concepts will allow us to construct new ways for men and women to come together so we can control the incidence and the effects of father hunger.

The "If–Only" Trap

When people adopt the "If only I were skinny" approach, they are trying to escape pain. Paradoxically, the problems I encounter in the eating-disordered patients, chronic dieters, compulsive eaters or exercisers, and weight–preoccupied women who enter my office, do not really have to do with weight and food. Those are merely the symptoms. The underlying issues are always rooted in the pain of past relationships. For many, fathers figure prominently as a source of discomfort and longing. Patients describe how they've always wanted to please their fathers, how they never felt they "measured up," how they used their bodies to gain affection or approval, or how they now eat too much or too little to deal with their sadness. These women have found a seemingly simple solution to the pain of disconnection from their fathers. "If only I were skinny," "If only I could stop eating" are their desperate refrains.

Our culture promotes the "If only I were skinny" solutions to this and many other problems. The media bombards us with messages equating thin, perfect bodies with wealth, success, status, and happiness. Such an environment suggests that the body size is the answer to interpersonal problems and negative emotions. These elaborate, seductive, shared fantasies are everywhere—on billboards, the radio, TV, in magazines, movies, books, and advertising. Their constant presence perpetuates the "if-only" trap and distorts our thinking and expectations.

"If-only" reasoning is a common way we express our desires. We want simple explanations. Assigning cause and effect in difficult situations helps us make sense of life and put order into an often confusing existence. It gives us a feeling of control, because it suggests that if we do a certain thing, we can change other things. A young woman thinks: "If I lose weight, daddy will respect me and be proud of me." Manipulating eating and body-size is seen as a socially-acceptable cure for her father hunger.

We must remember that "if-only" reasoning makes particular sense to children. In fact, until a stage in cognitive development called formal operations is reached, children naturally think in concrete terms and use reasoning patterns based on the linear A-causes–B, "if-only" relationships.[1] Only later are children able to conceptualize problems in a more complex manner. Instead of basing their solutions solely on concrete facts, they begin to draw upon abstract concepts.

People with food issues may be very intelligent, but their reasoning remains stuck in the concrete "if-only" approach when it comes to thinking through solutions to their sadness or low self-esteem. They are unable to recognize the cultural contributions to their feelings about their bodies or to their family's interactional patterns. Since it represents a return to the simplicity of childhood, "if-only" reasoning may be comfortable, but it can be dangerous as well.

The focus on food, weight, or body shape inherent in the "If only I were skinny" approach to life helps us avoid dealing with reality. It simplifies, distorts, and hides the underlying problems. By masking the real issues, this "if-only" approach actually prolongs the pain and sadness of disconnected relationships, especially with father. It keeps both father and daughter from facing their feelings and from confronting problems in the family's functioning and structure. It assigns all blame for father hunger on the daughter's body and her appetite for food. It promotes the belief that if her weight or eating change, her relationship with her father will be closer. Although she hopes to gain control by following her "if-only" reasoning through to the end, her methods ignore the real needs of her body. She will spend years hating herself for what she sees as her own lack of will power and her shameful body.

Parents or loved ones confronting someone with an eating disorder come up with their own set of "if-only" statements, such as "If only she would eat   .   .   .   ." or "If only she could like herself   .   .   ." They too must shift away from A-causes-B reasoning. Whether you are a person with a preoccupation about food, or a loved one trying to help, every time you find yourself saying "if only," you're going down the wrong road; you are simplifying and thus are avoiding underlying issues.

"If-onlys" imply one cause and one solution to a problem. Life is not that simple. There is only one "if only" that I ever heard that makes sense. When I asked one young woman who had recovered from her eating disorder if it could have been prevented, she answered:

> If only everything in my life and everything in my parents' lives had been different, then I guess I would not have had to be sick. But *everything* would have had to be different.

Relationships and Eating Problems: Systems Theory

We now can see why the old familiar A–causes–B, "if–only" reasoning does not work. To understand eating problems and father hunger, a different perspective is necessary. Systems theory is one that explains human behavior much more effectively. Simply put, it suggests that "the whole is greater than the sum of those parts," largely because of interactions among those parts.

When this theory is applied to families, it becomes apparent that father not only affects daughter, but everyone impacts everyone else, and all are influenced by systems outside the immediate family nucleus. These other systems include the myths and patterns established and carried over from earlier generations, the social environment and the demands it places on individuals, and the cultural roles assigned to each family member and to each sex.

When we apply systems theory to father hunger, we no longer simply blame fathers for their absence and their inability to support their daughters. Instead, we consider how our culture has evolved to limit this important link between men and women of different generations. The answers are not linear (how dad affects his daughter); they are systemic (how all members of the family and external influences interact).

Family systems theorists[2,3] best explain how all these factors interact and how different family patterns and problems occur. They describe the family as a cybernetic, dynamic system with all parts affecting each other through interactions, interconnections, and feedback. The components include: the individual's physical, biochemical, and psychological functioning; vulnerabilities from early development and psychological experience; family functioning and organization; multi-generational family patterns; developmental stresses on the individuals; and pressures from outside of the family.

In a system, no one part has unilateral control over another. Mara Selvini Palazzoli,[4] a well-known family therapist from Italy, points out that when one family member appears to cause another's behavior, it is really the cumulative effect of past interactional patterns within the whole family. Families develop "fixed behavioral responses" where one person may look like the villain or the cause of all the problems, when in fact, everyone in the system contributes to the pattern—no one person creates it.

For example, regarding the father's minimal role in the family, Palazzoli says, "The so-called ineffective father is a product of cooperation between all members of the system and not an intrapsychic fact." The women I meet who suffer from eating disorders indicate this in their own words when they describe how multi–generational family patterns or cultural trends have prescribed certain roles for their parents. In these family systems, the father was scripted to be peripheral and authoritative because the culture, family structure, and role assignment supported that role. Their fathers did not simply choose to be uninvolved.

The multi-generational patterns and external stressors include the traditions, myths, beliefs, and customary behaviors and roles that are accepted without question by a family. While myths and roles provide familiar structure, they may not fit the next generation and may create stress and pain for individuals in the present. Body-image dissatisfaction, problems with food, and eating disorders can be logical responses to these cultural and familial conflicts. Applying systems theory to your life may help you to overcome the "if-only" trap and to conceptualize how to address father hunger more effectively.

Fathers: A Potential Antidote to the "If Only I Were Skinny" Fantasy

Culture contributes to eating problems and body dissatisfaction in many complicated ways. Historically, women have been indoctrinated to concentrate on appearance and to alter themselves to please other people. Today, western culture places a high value on appearance, and thinness is equated with femininity and beauty. Furthermore, technology offers females many ways to attain the "perfect" body. Most experts in the field of eating disorders view these cultural and technological pressures on women to be thin as major reasons why so many young women are dieting and developing anorexia and bulimia.

Fathers can mediate the impact of these social dictates. For example, if a father agrees with our culture's shared fantasy that all your problems are solved if you have a perfect body, he will be contributing to the development of an eating disorder. However, a father can give his daughter other messages about beauty, self-worth, and body image that can counteract these strong cultural influences. Girls need a male adult to give corrective feedback and to balance the cultural pressures about being thin, sexy, and successful. Today, very young girls believe that "If only I were thin, people would like me more; Mommy and Daddy would be proud of me." If their fathers are not providing direct signs of acceptance and validation, young girls are apt to focus on their appearance and weight, hoping to gain dad's approval or attention.

Another cultural factor contributing to body dissatisfaction and weight preoccupation and to disruptions in the father-daughter relationship is the societal trend toward sexual behaviors in children and adolescents. The advances in birth control allow sexual activity without the risk of pregnancy, and our society no longer views intercourse among young teenagers as abnormal or unacceptable. The media also treats children as sexual beings at inappropriately young ages. Advertisements frequently show female children who are made to look grown-up, and more and more products originally intended for adults are aimed at children. For example, make-up is now marketed by cosmetics companies to nine- and ten-year-old girls because they have money to spend. The implication is that little girls need to do something to make themselves more appealing, prettier, or sexier.

Many little girls respond to these messages by becoming preoccupied with their appearance or by dressing in a provocative or adult style. Fathers often feel overwhelmed by this premature sexuality and may attempt to distance themselves from their daughters. Instead, they should find ways to remain close to their daughters as the girls experiment with these behaviors. Otherwise, girls may conclude that their fathers do not care or do not accept them and they may desperately attempt to change their bodies to either please dad or attract attention from other men.

For young women today, being thin has become the answer to a myriad of uncertainties they have about their lives and identities. During the latter half of the 20th century, women's roles in our culture have expanded dramatically. They are pursuing professions, interests, and lifestyles that previously were the exclusive domain of men. Many women in my generation live far different lives from what they expected, based on what their mothers' lives had been. Kim Chernin's book, *The Hungry Self: Women, Eating, and Identity*,[5] explores this concept in great detail, particularly the difficulties young women experience when they surpass their mothers. These revolutionary changes have contributed to inner turmoil and self-doubt, which in turn are being conveyed to today's little girls and adolescents.

Obsession with physical appearance and weight have become the primary means of dealing with this anxiety. "If only I were thin, then I'd be sure of myself" or "If only I were thin, other people would see me more positively." And today, the means available to change a woman's body are endless. Diet pills, diuretics, laxatives, special diets, liquid meals, make-up, fitness programs, spas, and plastic surgery all promise an answer to the uncertainties women are experiencing. Unfortunately, these technological answers to a lack of identity and feelings of confusion and low self-esteem are more available than nurturing relationships.

A father's positive messages can help his daughter face doubts she may have about what being a woman means today. He can help his daughter discern her life's direction, values, and identity. If he is supporting his wife emotionally and validating her work both at home and in the world, she'll be more positively involved with the family, and the children will see men and women working together effectively. When dad's role in the family is a constructive one, the daughter will not have to rely on the "If only I had a perfect body" fantasies in order to feel competent and successful as a woman and comfortable with her femininity. The more a daughter's father hunger has been satisfied, the less likely she will be to rely on the dangerous "if-onlys" that lead to body-image and eating conflicts as she attempts to forge her personal identity.

Recovery: The End to "If–Only" Reasoning

An essential step in recovering from an eating or body-image problem is understanding how we are influenced by our culture. This will make clear just how many different factors have contributed to these problems. Although the simplicity of the "if-only" reasoning is seductive, it cannot change anything. It points fingers and it blames, but because it does not try to understand and resolve, healing cannot occur. One woman who recovered from a severe eating disorder stated it this way:

> I used to love grade-school math. You can think things through and figure them out exactly. It works! I loved working at things like that. Recovery is kind of the opposite. It's like the end of all those easy math problems—you see things really aren't so simple.

I agree with her. Recovery is the end of the easy math problems. It is the beginning of figuring out how to change your own responses to situations that are beyond your control. The problems of the families in this book are too complex to attribute to "if-only" causes or solutions.

Eating problems are not simply signs of individual dysfunction. Although the individual with a preoccupation about food and body size has issues to address, the family structure and cultural expectations also need to change. With a heightened sensitivity to how our systems promote father hunger, we may be able to transform our society to one that will foster more satisfying relationships between fathers and daughters and prevent the pain caused by eating and body-image conflicts.

CHAPTER 2

TEN MYTHS ABOUT FATHERS, DAUGHTERS, AND FOOD

Myth #1:   Eating disorders and body image are women's issues.

Myth #2:   Men can't understand . . . . .

Myth #3:   Eating disorders are caused by problems in the mother/daughter relationship.

Myth #4   Distant, uninvolved fathers are the cause of eating disorders.

Myth #5:   Fathers play an inconsequential role in the development of their children.

Myth #6:   Father's role is to "provide" economically.

Myth #7:   Parenting isn't important to men.

Myth #8:   Fathers don't feel.

Myth #9:   Girls learn about femininity from their mothers.

Myth #10:   Girls need their mothers, not their fathers, during adolescence.

Myths are traditional legends or beliefs that guide our experience and help us make sense of the world. By definition, they may or may not have "a determinable basis of fact," and are "built up in response to the wishes of the group, rather than an analysis of the basis of the wishes."[1] These definitions indicate that myths are not necessarily hard facts but rather that they are reflections of our desires.

Social critics point out that our belief systems support the status quo by attributing current attitudes and related behaviors to ancient wisdom, natural laws, or sacred doctrines.[2] As a result, people are hesitant to question them and may even try to tailor their lives to fit into them. Myths give structure, reduce complex, overwhelming realities, and provide cause and effect explanations that make us feel better. They can be convenient and helpful, but when we stop questioning them and accept them as facts, they can be dangerous. When we conceptualize a myth as the only reality, we stifle our creativity, our problem solving, and our ability to adapt to new situations.

Today we maintain many outdated and destructive myths that underestimate the importance of fathers to their daughters. These beliefs promote father hunger and thereby encourage the eating and body-image conflicts that result from the disconnection of a daughter from her father. While mother/daughter struggles may be part of the background, women who develop eating problems have also been affected by their fathers. According to our myths, however, eating problems have little to do with a female's distance from her father and her struggle to understand and integrate masculinity and femininity in relationships; instead, they promote the belief that issues with food or body image come from problems between mothers and daughters, while fathers are just unimportant bystanders. These beliefs are so ingrained that until now, we have not explored the father's role in the development of food and body-image conflicts. It is time to be more critical and aware of the views we hold about families, roles, fathers, and female development.

Myth #1: **Eating disorders and body image are women's issues.**

Confronting many changes in social roles and expectations, both sexes are struggling to know how to relate to each other. Both experience conflicts as women attempt to achieve in previously masculine arenas. When these are not directly addressed, women often turn to food or their bodies to express their discomfort or to try to gain control. Thus, eating problems reflect women's discomfort in their relationships and their uncertainty about what is feminine and what is masculine.

The tension between the sexes today is particularly difficult for women, because relationships are so important to them. They will do almost anything to please others or to maintain a connection. This includes chronic dieting, starving, or waging war with their bodies. These are often misguided attempts to please, engage, satisfy, or attract men. In other cases, they are attempts to withdraw because of a fear of relationships with men.

Men also develop problems with food and their bodies. Are they suffering from a woman's issue? No, they're suffering from the same confusion about masculinity and femininity and about relationships as their female counterparts. Actually, many eating disorder experts believe that the number of men suffering from eating problems is greater than has been reported. Because we have defined eating disorders as a woman's issue, men who have similar behaviors are less likely to seek assistance. (In general, men have much more difficulty admitting that they have any kind of problem for which they need therapeutic assistance. Our culture teaches them to be strong, tough, unfeeling, and to need no one.) Men, also, have more acceptable ways to purge and to deal with their body-image problems. They can be obsessive in their exercise habits or they can choose to ignore fashion trends. Women do not generally see the latter as an option because they have been brought up to please others and to "be pretty." Today, however, men are meeting increasing social pressures to be thin and to change their eating habits. In the future, more of them may have problems with food and with body image.

Body dissatisfaction and problems with food plague both sexes, and the number of lives directly and indirectly affected by eating disorders continues to increase. Both men and women must face their contributions to the attitudes and behaviors that lead to body-image and eating problems.

Myth #2: **Men can't understand . . . . .**

Men can understand all kinds of complex things about women when given the information and the opportunity. Although there are distinct differences in how men and women process emotions, experience their bodies, and approach life, many of these develop or become exaggerated because of socialization, not because of biological uniqueness.

Women may perceive that "men can't understand" because the two sexes experience their bodies and food differently. Traditionally, men have been taught to accept their bodies no matter what shape they are in and to use them to *feel* good. In contrast, women have learned to be critical of their bodies and to suffer pain to *look* good. Both men and women function and interact without really knowing each other because they are following roles that dictate what each "should" be like. Neither understands the other, so men will often trivialize a woman's concerns about her body and women will say that men don't understand.

Men, however, are capable of understanding things from a woman's perspective if women try to communicate and interpret their experiences. Listening to women and learning from their struggles with their bodies would be particularly beneficial for men today. They too are being pressured to be fit, thin, strong, and in "perfect" aerobic condition, and are expected to expand their roles to include emotions and relationships. Both sexes have to abandon their cultural scripts and speak more from the heart to bridge the gap of misunderstanding between them.

Myth #3: **Eating disorders are caused by problems in the mother/daughter relationship.**

The fields of child development, abnormal psychology, and personality development overflow with theories about the negative impact of mothers on their children. The eating disorders literature is no exception to this. Because of the mother's central role as feeder and nurturer, theories have more often than not indicted mother as the villain. Eating problems really are not so simple; instead, they are a final common pathway for a myriad of issues. While the mother/child relationship is very powerful and may be problematic, many other factors also contribute. These include the functioning and emotional tone of the entire family system, the role of the father, the marital relationship, the patient's developmental problems, and the social and cultural context in which the family lives.

Cultural context is an especially important contributor to eating problems and body dissatisfaction. Ours has systematically devalued women, and recent attempts to correct this through the feminist movement often are accused of minimizing or even derogating the female attributes of nurturance and motherhood. As a society, we have overvalued the masculine virtues of strength and independence. The family structure mirrors this value system in both subtle and overt ways. Roles, rules, and relationships reflect the cultural context and thereby transmit social expectations, attitudes, and interaction patterns. Thus, a problem in an individual or between individuals in a family cannot be completely isolated from these other forces and from social changes.

While people with eating disorders often struggle with their relationships with their mothers, the conflict is much greater than that relationship alone. Although it is tempting to view this issue simplistically, eating disorders say more than "I'm having a problem with my mother."

Myth #4   Distant, uninvolved fathers are the cause of eating disorders.

If an uninvolved father truly were the exclusive cause, then we would have even more problems with food than we do! An uninvolved father is only one of many contributing factors. Attitudes that are deeply entrenched in the personal histories of the parents, their marital relationship, the functioning and scripts within the family, and individual stressors, all contribute and are compounded by the cultural emphasis on thinness, fitness, self-control, perfectionism, confusion about women's roles and femininity, and changes in the family structure. As in myth number three, many factors collide in the development of conflicts over eating and body image.

So, on these pages, you will not find support for the myth that "father is the villain." The father is a victim, as we all are, of myths, family structures, and social patterns that keep him outside the emotional life of the family and preclude a close relationship with daughters.

Myth #5:   Fathers play an inconsequential role in the development of their children.

This is an easy, attractive concept. It is perpetuated because our myths emphasize the necessity of the mother and the insignificance of the father in child rearing. However, the fact that men are not biologically able to give birth and to lactate does not mean that fathers are unimportant. When you reflect on the kind of person you have become, the things that hurt you, the defenses you use, and the things you value in life, can you really say your father was inconsequential in your development?

Many people reading this book had minimal relationships with their fathers, not necessarily because they or their fathers wanted this but because that's the way life was and continues to be. This distance, however, is not without consequences. It has a tremendous impact on self-esteem, identity, emotions, and behavior. Its effects will be expressed differently by each individual, but very often daughters will respond through their eating or their bodies.

If we keep telling ourselves that our fathers are inconsequential, this helps us avoid the pain, the disappointment, and the longing that we harbor for them. But if we allow ourselves to feel that pain—our father hunger—we may be able to get closer to the truth of our emotional lives and to our fathers.

Myth #6: **Father's role is to "provide" economically.**

Assigning the roles of provider to men and nurturer to women simply does not work, nor does it reflect the lives of many families today where parents share these responsibilities. For example, many women are single parents who provide financially for their children while maintaining the family's emotional life. Similarly, more and more divorced fathers are primary or custodial parents. Yet, we still hang onto the myth that mothers conduct the emotional business and fathers the economic business of the family. This attitude may have been accurate centuries ago when social forces such as the industrial revolution and the division of labor moved father into the work place and mother into the role of homemaker and nurturer. But, as our roles have changed, so our myths need to change as well.

Until we foster new myths, many people will try hard to comply with the old ones. Consequently, men may be threatened when their spouses gain financial power. Women may feel insecure when their husbands try to be more actively involved in the family. The dichotomy between economic and emotional roles in the family is unfair to everyone. The belief that a man's priority should be to make more money and to "provide" for the family restricts men's ability to give emotionally and to be spontaneously involved in the family's life. It denies children any access to their father as a person and does not show them how men and women can work together and share power, responsibility, and caring. It tells mother that she alone is responsible for the emotional life of the family and that her other interests or work are secondary or unimportant.

Clearly, no one benefits from our current mythology. Even though this myth is no longer accurate, we continue to stress father's role as breadwinner and to create obstacles to the sharing of responsibilities that many couples attempt.

Myth #7: **Parenting isn't important to men.**

This myth is particularly deceptive and damaging. Therapists have long recognized that when a man becomes a father the experience is one of the most profound and gut-wrenching in his life. Parenting presents many issues for men. It forces them to confront feelings and situations for which they feel totally unprepared. Fatherhood implies instant adulthood and responsibility. This is a difficult developmental step because most men have been cared for by their mothers and wives for years. All of a sudden they are responsible for a baby and a whole family. While the new father is trying to cope with this, the infant completely dominates his wife's attention. He often feels inept and abdicates much of the caregiving to his wife. Furthermore, since society limits dad's role to that of economic provider, it gives him few opportunities to build full relationships with his children as they grow.

These situations and dynamics often cause a father to feel ignored, lonely, inadequate, and unimportant. Although he may desperately want to be involved, he may not know how. To further complicate his emotions, the transition to fatherhood brings up unfinished business left over from past experiences with his own father. The new father may become aware of how his dad was absent in his childhood and how he felt fatherless and hungry for more of a relationship. Some may react to this realization by feeling more alone and overwhelmed, while others may be over-joyed with the prospect of being an active father. Men obviously have a variety of responses to fatherhood—a life stage that evokes mixed feelings of self-doubt, strong achievement orientation, anxiety, nurturance, dreams, and a desire for intimacy.

We have assumed that parenting is not important to men because they fit so neatly and obediently into the role of "pro-vider." Isn't it about time we started caring about how fathers feel? What would happen if we told men that being affected by parenthood is acceptable? What would happen if we encouraged fathers to talk about this? Quite simply, we would find out how significant the experience of fatherhood is to most men.

Myth #8: **Fathers don't feel.**

It might be more accurate to say that men displace and deny their feelings, rather than that they don't have any. This pattern is the result of years of socialization that, starting in infancy, teaches them not to feel or cry but to go out into the world and conquer it. Men grow up not knowing how to recognize, accept, and sort out their emotions and their need for intimacy. As a result of years of denial, they become out of touch with their bodies as well. They don't listen to the cues that they're doing too much or not taking care of themselves, and thus, they suffer from stress-related illnesses (hypertension, ulcers, cardiac dysfunction, substance abuse) more frequently than women do. In fact, one reason why life expectancy in the United States is seven to eight years shorter for men[3] may be this high stress level. "Stress" represents mis-placed emotions, so men may be feeling much more than we recognize.

Although we try to believe the myth that men do not feel, most of us can remember seeing tears in our father's eyes, but the tears froze there because men were told never to show them. We have seen our fathers distressed while pretending to be nonchalant and in control, but we deny this in order to maintain our outdated myths. Thus, we perpetuate these limiting roles for men.

It's clear that men have feelings. We need to find ways for all of us to be comfortable with them. Frank Pittman, a family therapist, described men's emotional dilemmas with the following metaphor: "Hypermasculinity is armor—it's just a protective coating—a shell, like mussels, clams, lobster, or shrimp. Just beneath the shell, the meat may be sweet."[4]

Myth #9: **Girls learn about femininity from their mothers.**

The theories about child development and the formation of self identity traditionally have emphasized the importance of the same-sex parent. In other words, to develop into adult men and women boys need their fathers and girls need their mothers. It isn't quite this simple, however. Children need both their parents. Interacting with the opposite-sex parent helps youngsters to understand what is unique or important about their own sex. A girl will understand some of the important aspects of femininity by knowing about masculinity. Her father can be an important teacher of this.

A girl develops beliefs about feminine behavior by watching her father interact with women. She observes the traits he values, the behavior that evokes his support or his disdain, and the way he treats them. A father's treatment of his wife especially influences the adolescent daughter in her struggle to determine the ways in which she should be similar to, or different from, her mother. This is part of the separation and individuation process, or differentiation of self, and it involves the father as much as the mother.

As they grow up, both girls and boys may see their fathers as being more involved outside of the family than their mothers. Although their mothers may also have important roles outside the family, children usually see them operating inside the family.

Consequently, fathers' views of the adult world and life beyond the home front hold special meaning and importance to the rest of the family. They represent a world viewpoint, and so daughters may look more to their fathers—and less to their mothers—for cultural opinions, definitions, and beliefs about femininity. Today, because women's roles have changed tremendously and are still in flux, girls need as much direction and guidance as they can get from both the significant women and the significant men in their lives.

Myth #10: **Girls need their mothers, not their fathers, during adolescence.**

Again, girls require both their father and their mother; it's not an either/or choice. Especially when parents are separated or divorced, girls need contact with both parents and should not have to choose one over the other. Mothers must accept their daughter's interest in their father and their husband's interest in their daughters. While young boys who lose contact with their father show the impact of this loss early, the effect is generally not apparent in girls until adolescence or adulthood, when they became aware of their own sexuality and are expanding their personal and social relationships with men.[5]

Fathers play a particularly special role in their daughter's passage from childhood to adolescence. Girls need to be "courted" by their fathers, in a non-seductive way, to move from being girls to becoming young women. They want to feel attractive, womanly, and acceptable to the most important men in their lives (their fathers). This helps them accept their changing bodies and gives them confidence with boys. When this acceptance does not occur, girls often experience self-doubt, self-deprecation, and depression. They may act out their distress in different ways—by withdrawing from social contact, by being promiscuous, or by the self-loathing and rejection of self that is expressed through an eating disorder.

Adolescent girls experience a loss of their father's attention for many reasons. Because fathers are told they're unimportant to their children, particularly to their daughters, they may not devote the energy necessary to work at the changing relationship that naturally occurs when girls leave childhood and become adolescents. Fathers frequently do not enjoy their daughters' new interests and the attention they pay to appearance and to the intricate details of their relationships. Their daughters no longer seek them out for childhood games and bedtime stories, so fathers may not know how to reach out and interact with them. Thus, developing a more sexual body and becoming a young woman may be associated with the loss of their father. When growing up means losing significant relationships, the process is not attractive or promising.

On the positive side, numerous studies have shown that women who report having had a close and caring relationship with their father during childhood developed a strong sense of personal identity and positive self-esteem. Female college students who perceived their dads as being nurturant, emotionally available, and interested in their development, scored well on personal adjustment; those with rejecting fathers scored poorly. College women who identified with their fathers were found to be more autonomous, and females with involved and attentive fathers have more successful male/female relationships as adults.[6]

Fathers need to be available to their daughters to make their development a positive process, to lure them forward to adulthood. This helps young women integrate their own sexual maturity into the relationship with their fathers and with men in general. It provides continuity between childhood and later development and makes the new experiences, challenges, and responsibilities of adolescence and adulthood feel more safe. Most importantly, it assures them that their dads still love them. Daughters need this assurance no matter how old they are.

To fully address the issues and consequences of father hunger, changes and healing must occur not only on the individual and family, level but also culturally. Although the current myths and roles for men and women in families have created a minimal part for fathers, they work well; that is, they serve a functional purpose. For this reason, families adhering to cultural traditions appear to function well on a superficial level, but these limiting roles and rules contribute to much personal dissatisfaction and family dysfunction.

We need to challenge the notions and myths that accept these imbalanced roles and promote father hunger in each succeeding generation. This will require creative changes in the scripts of both men and women, in the home as well as the work environment, to redistribute power and responsibility more evenly in families. Take some time to do the following "Food for Thought" exercise. Then think more about new myths that could promote a deeper, closer relationship between children and their fathers and that would gradually decrease the epidemic and long-term consequences of father hunger.

Questions and New Connections

•   How many of the myths did you agree with before you read this chapter? How many do you agree with now?

•   How have these myths affected your life and your relationship with your father?

•   How would our lives change if fathers were more available and involved in the family?

CHAPTER 3

◆ ◆ ◆

FATHERS AS
SECOND–CLASS CITIZENS

American traditions and myths have treated men as second-class citizens or shadows in families. Michael Lamb, one of the first researchers to examine the role of the father, states that this devaluation has systematically caused children in the United States to "suffer effective paternal deprivation."[1] This chapter examines the evolution of the father's role throughout earlier cultural environments and social structures. To understand today's father, we have to understand his forefathers. Since a society's economic base, structure, and historical events shape people's interactions, patterns, and sex roles, we must scrutinize how the sociocultural framework helps or hinders the father's role.

The feminist movement has provided a voice for many women who have felt degraded by the culturally-ascribed roles they hold. It has enabled them to challenge these restrictions, expand themselves, and feel valued and respected for their overall importance to society. Until now, men as a group have lacked a cultural force. Very recently, however, a men's movement has emerged,[2] and, if strong enough, it could eventually reverse the father hunger that pervades and undermines the contemporary family.

In every culture, there exists some division of labor or demarcation of roles according to sex. Even ancient writings indicate that fathers played a more remote role than mothers, describing them as stern, wise, authoritative and uninvolved with the family or children. As we trace the evolution of the father through the 20th century, we continue to see fathers being less available and more authoritarian than mothers.[3] Today, however, we are experiencing significant discomfort about the script for men in families. As a result of this, there is a great potential for change.

FATHER'S ROLE IN THE FAMILY: A HISTORICAL PERSPECTIVE

One of the earliest social structures that has been studied extensively is the hunting and gathering society. On an initial comparison of this group with ours, we might think that these fathers were less available than in today's families because of their long absences in search of food. However, if we examine this society more closely, our preliminary conclusion is not supported. In these communities, fathers could be completely absent for periods of time. But as soon as the hunt was over, they returned home. Men were absent only to obtain the basic essentials their families needed. The length of time they were away was dependent on the season, the weather, or other factors.

Actually, the hunting and gathering family was not deprived of contact with paternal figures. They experienced few family problems when father was absent because of the structure and support given to both parental roles. When father was present, he was available and involved, instructing his sons to hunt and conveying the society's customs to his children. Older men, no longer strong enough to hunt, stayed behind, teaching survival skills as they helped to raise the children. Essentially, men were visible and active in the family.

Despite the distinct division of labor, the two sexes shared power. For example, when men were away, women were given undisputed authority, and their role as gatherer and preparer of food was acknowledged as essential to survival. Men were welcomed back to camp and were appreciated for their contributions, both when they were present and when they were absent. In these ways, division of labor actually crystallized and supported each sex's role. Men and women enjoyed a more egalitarian existence than in later times. Because the subsistence societies were classless, issues of power and control between the sexes were not as critical as they eventually became. Men and women were equally involved with the family and equally important contributors as parents.

The family structure and sex roles changed significantly with the transition from subsistence-based hunting and gathering to more agrarian societies. Since agricultural work requires great physical strength, men became the active farmers and women no longer worked alongside their mates. Permanent houses and villages replaced the nomadic living of hunters and gatherers. Women cared for the children and developed the home environment, while men worked long, grueling hours as farmers. Youngsters interacted minimally with their fathers until they were strong enough to work on the farm. The agrarian era, with its consequent impact on parental roles, may have initiated the father hunger of modern society.

The transition to an agricultural subsistence brought with it the potential for surplus supplies, which in turn created the ability to earn income and gain power. Farmers could accumulate supplies, and wealth and class were based more on men's work than on the joint effort of men and women working together. The family structure was becoming more patriarchal, with men less immediately involved in family life but more active as decision-makers. While women had the responsibility for children and the home, men had authority because of their potential wealth and social status. One writer who has chronicled the evolution of the father's role believes that men had a strong need to assume authority in the family as they progressed from being hunters to farmers. As he says, "The hunter dominates his prey, whereas the farmer governs his family."[4]

During this agrarian period, newly-married couples usually moved onto the property of the husband's family. This move by the wife to her husband's family symbolized the man's authority. Fathers became increasingly inaccessible to children but retained power outside of the family and thus became remote patriarchs. Later, with urbanization, land became less important and couples tended to move to the wife's family home after marriage. Fathers, still removed from the family's daily life, lost some influence with this change and their status in the family began to weaken.

IMPACT OF THE INDUSTRIAL REVOLUTION

The industrial revolution was probably the most significant factor in the evolution and decline of the father's role in families. Until this time, the father's work was in and around the home. Children saw their fathers and other men during the day and had some concept of their father's work. With industrialization, however, men started working long hours away from home and became nearly invisible to their children. Mothers assumed the main responsibility for child-rearing. Although the father's role had traditionally stressed teaching moral and religious values as well as survival skills such as hunting or farming, his script soon became primarily to provide economically for the family, to "bring home the bacon," to be the breadwinner. The switch from a nonindustrial to an industrial society moved father out of the home and changed the family environment dramatically.

Changes in fashion and physical adornment reflected this transformation of men's and women's roles. Prior to industriali-

zation, men and women equally pursued beauty, physical adornment, and fashion. (Look at paintings from the Renaissance to
remind yourself of this. Men were extremely fashion-conscious at
that time. They wore wigs, makeup, and pampered themselves as
much as women did.) Once men began to work in factories,
though, they started to dress more plainly. To demonstrate the
fruits of their labor—their money, power, and status—men became interested in adorning their wives. Historically, women had
always altered their appearance to please others, but with the
industrial revolution, the wife's appearance and her adherence to
fashion now expressed the husband's status. The increased emphasis on female beauty is one of the negative outcomes of the
shifts in men's and women's roles that accompanied industrialization which contributes to today's obsession with body image.[5]

As the industrial revolution proceeded, the fields of education,
child development and psychology also emerged. They emphasized the importance of motherhood and all but ignored fatherhood, while the emerging lifestyle lent increasing support to the
growing myth that children need their mothers exclusively. Fathers were seen as extraneous. Still responsible for moral education and for the dirty work of disciplining, their role was limited
to one of judge, policeman, and breadwinner, effectively under-
mining their relationships with their children. This put the father
in an untenable position; it moved him out of the family and left
intact only his role as economic provider and disciplinarian.

We are still experiencing the after-shocks of industrialization.
Before examining the more recent trends, let's summarize the
important effects of these economic and social changes. The
industrial revolution removed the father from a visible role in the
family and began the movement of raising fatherless children.
Success outside of the home became the primary goal for men.
Women had sole responsibility for child-rearing and their beauty
and appearance became a means to convey their husband's success. Highly differentiated scripts for men and women limited the

intimacy, trust, and expression of emotions in families. These cultural patterns laid the groundwork for eating and body-image problems that plague so many women today.

THE 20TH–CENTURY FATHER

Our culture's myths and expectations have placed the 20th-century father in a double-bind. He can't win! For a man to be a "good father," he has to be *outside* the family. In fact, in the latter half of the 20th century, the more a father removes himself from the family to do his work, the better he fulfills his role as provider. This view of father is reflected in Dr. T. Berry Brazelton's advice to parents in the early 1970s in his column for *Redbook* magazine. Brazelton states that a man's work outside the home is the "very core of his position in the family" and that his absence should be treated as an indication of his love and commitment to it.[6] Since children need concrete and physical evidence of affection and caring, however, they often feel ignored and insecure when dad doesn't spend time with them. This is the dilemma in which the modern American father has found himself. What a Catch 22! The more a father does away from his family, the better father he is, even if his kids hardly know him!

Until the late 1920s and early 1930s, the father's role as breadwinner and disciplinarian continued as the unchallenged prototype. The Great Depression, however, dealt a significant blow to the self-esteem and identity of American men. Despite all their hard work and the money they had acquired, they could no longer provide economically for their families. Being the bread-winner had been the core of their identity because they had little, if any, other function in the family. Many men either lost their jobs or worked far fewer hours and became quite depressed; some committed suicide while others numbed themselves with alcohol. Although fathers might have been home more, they probably were not emotionally present for their families.

Since then, we have seen fathers disenfranchised and unhappy, weary of the pressure to support the family financially with minimal access to the family's emotional life. Some authors speculate that the pressures placed on fathers to achieve in their roles, together with our lack of emotional support, have contributed to the Type-A personality and stress-related illnesses that we see so frequently in males.[7] Their fate during the 20th century has caused some men to begin to question the wisdom of defining themselves and their lives almost exclusively through their work.

World War II was the next major influence on the American family. By the late 1930s, the American economic scene had begun to improve, primarily due to the war. Factories were operating at full force on defense contracts and fathers were once again able to provide for their families. When the United States assumed an active role, women assumed the industrial jobs and men left to fight overseas. The climate was one of support for the war and acknowledgment of men's crucial responsibility to protect their families and the world from the destructive forces of Naziism and Imperialism. The father's importance outside the home was once more supported and endorsed. During this period, the roles of both sexes stabilized in the United States. The war strengthened the American woman's position, as now she had to maintain both the family and the country's economy. An aura of mutual respect and support developed.

After the war, however, many women experienced a loss of status when they were again relegated to the role of homemaker. Men resumed their distance from the family to take advantage of postwar economic opportunities. During this time of consolidation, the family was highly valued, sex roles were rigidly defined, and father's task was to succeed at work, while mother's was to take care of the family. Father remained the disciplinarian, moral teacher, and provider, but a new trend emerged for him which was to be a strong role model for his sons,[8] setting a standard of economic and vocational success, personal strength, self-control, and reserved, non-emotional logic. Daughters were encouraged to model their mother's behavior, which emphasized homemaking and family harmony, so scripts for men and women were highly divergent.

Despite these significant changes, life was fairly complacent for families after World War II. This was certainly the calm before the storm. By the late 1960s, the conflicts brewing during this tranquil period would challenge all of the traditional family values and roles. The two key events contributing to this unrest were the Vietnam War and the Women's Movement.

American involvement in the Vietnam War stimulated extreme intergenerational conflict, divisiveness and persistent doubts about the wisdom of male authority figures. The anti-war movement, largely composed of college students, challenged the establishment's position more loudly and forcefully than any other group had ever challenged a war. The younger generation rejected the decisions and power of their fathers and openly questioned the morality and values of both parents. The rift that developed between the two generations led to an almost complete rejection of traditional values and customs. It was not an easy time for parents who had worked hard to provide their children with material wealth and security. The older generation, which had grown up accepting war as a fact of life and believing in the importance of the United States as a safeguard of democracy, could not understand youth's incessant questioning and disputes over the morality and purpose of America's role in southeast Asia. Many still have unhealed wounds from the intergenerational conflicts brought on by the war in Vietnam.

Families continue to feel the effects of this war in other ways. Many veterans have suffered long-term consequences to their psyche and self-esteem. Because of the strong opposition to this war, some vets have felt ashamed of their participation, while others are proud but angry that their contributions have not been recognized. Some vets worry about their exposure to chemicals (primarily Agent Orange) and the effects it may have on their children's long-term health. Veterans and protestors alike are haunted by conflicts and flashbacks of their experiences. Some have developed psychological or substance-abuse problems as they wrestle with the war's ongoing impact on their lives. These issues have made it difficult for many men to feel effective and positive as fathers.

While the Vietnam War stimulated the possibility for change and the urgent need to examine our values as a society, the Women's Movement, rekindled in the late 1960s, further prompted us to look at sex roles in a different light. The effect of this movement has been to slowly reorganize society to allow women more room to perform outside of the family and men more room to perform within it. Many young men who rejected the war and were disgusted by their fathers' values, began to see traditional masculinity as a negative and evil symbol. They were attracted to the women's movement because it questioned the culturally accepted male roles.[9]

There are other factors contributing to the possibility for change in fathers' roles within the family. Although the pressure is still on fathers to work hard and provide well, men generally work fewer hours than they did 100 years ago. Actually, men are being forced to function more actively in the family, because women are pursuing jobs and looking for broader fulfillment. A compelling example of this was when American women participated as active soldiers in our most recent war, the Persian Gulf conflict, and fathers were left at home to take care of the children. As women continue to experience the more traditionally male side of life, men will be able to experience more of their nurturing female side. But we need to support both sexes through these changes.

The end of the 20th century presents men with opportunities for more involvement with their families, but this transformation is not going to be easy. Most men still see work as the key to their identity, and they experience conflicts between family life and their jobs. Employers expect men to travel and to sacrifice personal time to advance or even to maintain their positions. Men will often accept exhaustive demands at work because supporting the family economically remains crucial to male self-concept and self-esteem, and to being a "good enough" father. Furthermore, many jobs today require advanced technical skills, are personally isolating, and require aggressive behaviors that are not compatible with family life. The competitive, win-lose mentality, and quick, logical decisions that bring success in the office often are disastrous skills at home.

The increased number of women in the work force also creates uneasiness. As men find themselves competing with women, they may feel intimidated or angry. Although most grew up in families in which husbands were encouraged to be workaholics and wives were supposed to support them no matter what, they can no longer expect this. Instead, they may find women competing with them at work and demanding more of them at home. As a result, they feel confused, unsuccessful, threatened, and unsupported in both environments.

Men are truly struggling today in their roles in the American family. Most were raised traditionally with an involved mother and an absent father. They grew up expecting the same kind of life, but are confronted by wives who are challenging this and are unhappy with the old ways of being in a marriage. With all that has transpired in the 20th century, most men want their role to encompass more than just providing materially for the family, but there are no maps showing the way to this new land of fathering.

What is Fathering?

Unfortunately, the methods, hypotheses, and trends in traditional psychological research have supported the notion of the father as a second–class citizen and continued the cycle of father hunger. We know little about fathering because, until very recently, we have completely ignored this important human behavior.

Freud showed a nearly exclusive interest in the mother-child relationship and thereby set the tone for how psychology and psychiatry came to view fathers. Although he acknowledged that the father's protection of his children is the "central childhood imperative"[10] and that the father's death is the most significant event in a man's life, he never addressed the nurturing, or generative, aspects of fathering. Later in the 20th century, John Bowlby, who wrote seminal works on the attachment and bonding process of young children, also concentrated on the mother-child relationship, and relegated the father's function to the "economic and emotional support of the mother."[11] As the fields of psychology and child development flourished in the mid-20th century, the practicalities of the research process lent support to the emphasis on mother-infant relationships. Conceptually, studying dyadic (one-to-one) relationships is much easier than studying how the whole family system interacts. And, since research is generally done during the day, when fathers are at work, mothers were often the only parent available. So, consciously or unconsciously, mental health theories served to maintain the myth that fathers are unimportant.

Only in the past 20 years have researchers become interested in the father and his role in child development. Several factors have stimulated this closer look. First, the prevailing sociocultural conditions served as important catalysts. By the 1970s, the traditional family structure began to change dramatically, the divorce rate had increased, and many homes had no fathers physically present. Consequently, the impact of paternal absence became a primary research interest. Reflecting the myths about father-child relationships, however, most studies examined the impact of father absence on boys, but ignored its effect on girls.

A number of other trends accelerated our interest in the father's role in the family. Many divorced fathers made tremendous efforts to be actively involved in their children's lives despite their absence from the home. Also, we realized that children can develop strong relationships with caregivers other than mothers. Finally, infant research indicated that babies were more than passive recipients of interactions and hypothesized that we had underestimated their ability to develop relationships.

At the same time these discoveries were made, the mental health field, waking up to the fact that there is no single and separate influence on a child's development, began to appreciate the complexity and the contribution of the larger family environment. Simple concepts such as the mother-child relationship no longer sufficed to explain a child's behavior. Therapists recognized that the parents' relationship with each other had an important effect on their children. New work in adult development found that the experience of parenting affects both men and women. All of these factors converged to pave the way toward a new appreciation of the father's significance in the family.

Once we broadened our vision to include the possibility that the father is important to his children, the resulting research revealed many interesting things. In 1974, two physicians wrote a paper about the newborn's impact on the father, a phenomenon they called "engrossment."[12] According to their observations, within the first few days of the infant's life, the father develops a bond, or gets "hooked" on the child. They observed, however, that few social supports are available to help a father maintain this connection and to feel comfortable around the baby. The fathers they studied also reported feeling a definite sense of accomplishment and an enhanced self-image with the birth of their children.

Being a parent awakens many startling and strong emotions for men. One father of an infant recently described his feelings as "fireballs of love [that] swoop through him all the time," so that he "feels like the Fourth of July is happening inside him."[13] This writer shows us that when men allow themselves to experience it, fathering can help them discover wonderful parts of themselves they would not otherwise know.

Even before the birth, fathers can become very involved in the psychological preparation for parenting. Expectant fathers often worry a great deal and experience anxiety and mood changes. One fourth of the expectant fathers in a study of normal pregnancies, sought medical help for gastrointestinal symptoms they had never before experienced. In some more primitive societies, the phenomenon of couvade (when the man simulates labor and delivery) is very common. The husband's parallel physical process supposedly eases his wife's pain and protects her and the baby during the birth process.[14]

The father-child relationship can be established fairly early in a child's life and is as important to the infant as it is to the father. Infants are strongly attached to their fathers by the age of nine months.[15] In fact, because of the differences in each parent's style of interacting with the infant, fathers may have a unique and crucial part in the child's socialization. Mothers caretake and teach. They tend to be more conventional, predictable, and goal-directed than fathers. While mothers feed, bathe, and change diapers, fathers play with infants in a physical, stimulating, action-oriented way. Babies begin to connect the father with fun, adventure, new experiences, and spontaneity. They are easily interested in dad, and a reciprocal relationship will develop if circumstances allow.

The work of anthropologists is enlightening as we try to help men be more active parents. Several who have examined fathering have found it to be a plastic or moldable behavior, very much affected by the environment. William Redican's studies of other primates[16] led to the discovery that fathering is present in some species where it is totally unexpected, even in very independent and aggressive male animals. He concludes that fathering is an innate capacity and that its presence largely depends on whether opportunities and encouragement are given to express it.

Anthropologists Mary West and Melvin Konner[17] examined various human cultures and have drawn similar conclusions. They point out that no singular, natural, or correct way of fathering exists, and that its expression will either be enhanced or denied by the cultural role prescribed for men and women. West and Konner found the greatest degree of paternal involvement in cultures where local warfare is absent, spousal relationships are monogamous, the division of labor allows fathers access to children, and women's work other than child-care is considered important. Maybe we can learn something from West and Konner's work. Fathering is present when men and women are working together effectively as partners. It sounds easy, doesn't it?

This recent research on the father-child relationship disproves the myth that the instinct to parent is stronger in, or the exclusive prerogative of, women. In fact, parenting skills develop "on the job." Mothers become experts by practicing. Likewise, fathers do not, although they can develop the reciprocal attachment we associate with good mothering. Children with involved fathers have been found to have higher cognitive and developmental functioning, greater empathy, a stronger internal locus of control, and less rigid sex stereotypes.[18] A study of 17 families in which fathers were the primary caregivers found that the babies were more socially responsive and above average developmentally.[19] When fathers have to, choose to, or are encouraged to, they can take care of infants. While they may express their parenting differently, both parents have the capacity to nurture and care for children. Fathers can be first-class parents, instead of second-class citizens.

CULTURAL SUPPORT FOR FATHERS: PRESENT OR ABSENT?

Unfortunately, feeling secure and supported in their parenting is an elusive goal for both men and women of today. The mass media and pop psychology, two new influences in the latter half of the 20th century, constantly bombard us with the latest trends and best techniques for child rearing. Every newspaper and magazine we pick up has a new theory to substitute for the personal guidance parents used to receive from their extended families when they were a single unit. Expert opinions are always changing, however, and may not fit the needs of the individuals involved.

Susie Orbach, a feminist psychotherapist, has written extensively about the sociocultural contributions to eating disorders. She believes that the constantly changing trends regarding appropriate or optimal child-rearing have contributed to an insidious insecurity in parents, which in turn contributes to eating disorders. She states, "The rigidity of the syndrome is a symbolic attempt to forge a consistency where little exists, to provide a knowledgeable, reliable way of being that can withstand the demand for change."[20]

Both men and women are confused about parenting, and while this confusion may produce problems such as eating disorders, it has the potential to produce positive changes for the family as well. Some favorable adjustments have already occurred. As a culture, we have begun to acknowledge that fathers can and should nurture others and that parents should share in raising children. We have started to examine and endorse father's rights in custody cases and in paternity leaves. While these changes promote the possibility of more active fathering, we also have a rising divorce rate and a resulting breakdown in the father-child relationship. With an increase in females as heads of households, millions of children in the United States are being raised without fathers. This is a critical time for fathers and for families. We must break the pattern of father hunger. Children need both men and women in their lives. We have to make dad less of a mystery and more available to his family. We need to stop the cultural demotion of the father to the role of second-class citizen.

Questions and New Connections

•   Imagine what your relationship with your father would be like if you lived in a different historical period. What cultural supports were available to fathers during that time?

•   What can employers do to make men more available to their families? What impact would paternity leave and flexible working hours have on children and families?

•   How should custody and visitation plans be designed to allow access to fathers?

CHAPTER 4

A SHAKY FOUNDATION
FOR FATHERHOOD:
Male Psychological Development

Fathers and adolescent daughters each have worries, dreams, insecurities, needs, drives, and desires that may have been dormant, more manageable, or less important during the girl's earlier years. When she becomes a teenager, however, the differences or conflicts between them become accentuated. Adolescence challenges the equilibrium between the sexes as well as between the generations. This is the time when many fathers and daughters experience a complete breakdown in their relationship, leading young women to long for paternal affection and approval—to hunger for daddy.

Fathering an adolescent daughter is difficult for both parties. Father and daughter may be equally bothered by unfinished business from their childhoods and by the changes brewing as they face a new life-stage. As the father makes the transition to mid-life, he will be re-examining his goals and values. He may decide to alter his life in some significant way, causing his daughter confusion at the same time that she is dealing with the chaos of adolescence. Or he may become very rigid, unable to adjust to the challenges and needs of a teenager. On the other hand, the daughter is forming her identity, and in this vulnerable stage she brings an uncertain sense of self to the relationship. She needs support, security, and acceptance, especially from the most important man in her life. Unfortunately, fathers are often ill-prepared to provide these things.

The differences between the male and female "psyche," which contribute to father hunger and which are so evident in families with eating problems, begin at birth and become firmly rooted by early childhood. Some psychologists might say that the differences precede birth because they are derived from the collective unconscious and human history; or the attitudes, expectations, and personal experiences of the parents; or the physiological variations in development and functioning.

However, regardless of when they begin or why they occur, socialization and cultural experience are powerful influences on men and women. I agree with feminist psychologists who believe that current sociocultural conditions are "developmentally disabling to young females."[1] But these are also disabling to young men. Men grow up devoid of deep connections and particularly deprived of meaningful relationships with father figures. Neither sex appears to be getting a healthy or an easy start in life. In our current manner of raising children, each sex seems to be disenfranchised, incomplete, and unsupported by the other.

This chapter will explore how the psychological development of males in western society affects fathering and repeats the cycle wherein men who have been deprived of contact with their fathers cannot effectively nurture the next generation. Parenting girls is particularly challenging for men because of the differences between their skills and their daughters' needs.

THE MESSAGE TO MEN:
SEPARATE, SEPARATE, SEPARATE!

The differentiation of self or the creation of an individual identity provides the basis of personality formation which involves the primary caretaker to a great extent. It is a complex and lifelong process. In western culture, this is usually the mother, and so the progression unfolds differently in boys than in girls and will have divergent consequences later in life, affecting personal adjustment, the marital relationship, and parenting.

For boys, developing an identity and differentiating oneself means separating from the warmth and cuddling of mom and connecting to dad, a more remote, less demonstrative, and often more demanding parent. This process is difficult because of the special relationship between mothers and male infants. Studies show that they allow sons more opportunity to play with their food and to develop their own feeding schedule, while they make their daughters adjust more to external demands, such as being neat and eating on schedule. Mothers wean and toilet train males later than females.[2] Thus, the mother-son relationship could be seen as indulgent, or at least as very special and loving.

The indulgence experienced by most males during infancy creates difficulties later when they go through the phases of development that require separation. In contrast to the earlier cuddling, mothers are now pushing their sons "out of the nest." When mothers encourage them toward independence, sons instinctively understand the need to be separate and independent. Still, the loss of mom can be very traumatic, and father's absence, his disinterest, or his rejection, will intensify it. A strong connection with dad can help boys cope with this change in the relationship with mom.

Also, men are generally unavailable to children in our society. Many boys never experience encouragement, affection, support, and intimacy in relationships with any adult males. These may not know how to seek support. They may grow up not even knowing how to have close friendships with their same-sex peers.

After losing the warm relationship with mother and being unable to find intimacy with men, boys grow up with many unmet emotional needs. These are generally tabled until they establish a meaningful relationship with a woman, because men are often only comfortable expressing or seeking affection through sex. Being held and loved may help them to reconnect with earlier points in their development when they felt cared for by their mothers.

This unfinished business and disappointment in the male's relationship with his parents will also affect his adult behavior as a father. For example, if a man only feels close to women via a physical relationship, he may not know how to remain close to his daughter as she matures sexually. Many fathers choose to distance themselves from their daughters to avoid this uneasiness. Other men, whose needs for connection can only be satisfied by the female nurturance they have missed since early childhood, may become overly dependent on their daughters. They may inadvertently make their daughters into second mothers or wives or even pursue a sexual relationship with them.

We shall understand the male's unmet needs better if we think about the messages we give to little boys as we push them to separate and develop. From infancy on we tell them: "Be a big boy," "Stand on your own two feet," "Be tough," "Don't cry," "It doesn't hurt," among many other invalidating messages. We teach little boys not to to be aware of, or at least, not to express their emotions, and we tell them not to need anything from anyone.

These constant directives leave them feeling empty, alone, scared, and vulnerable, but they aren't supposed to experience such sentiments, so they pretend nothing is wrong. Little boys pick up early that emotions are "feminine"—only for "sissies." Since they are learning how to be "masculine," they begin to devalue feelings and to disown their needs. In this way, we actually encourage boys to separate not only from both parents, but also from their own inner emotional lives.

THE COST OF SEPARATION: "NO SATISFACTION"

Tracing the psychological and social pressures males experience as they grow up will help us to understand why they so rarely find satisfaction in themselves or in their relationships. Surrounded by messages that belittle male emotional expressions, boys are unable to let others know how sad and alone they feel as they separate from mom and try to identify with and model dad. They recognize their fathers' strength and power in the world but also perceive a man who functions minimally in the family and who is often emotionally and socially inadequate. Since fathers can't admit to these "weaknesses," sons deny their perceptions and cover up their own weak or needy feelings by trying anything to get contact with and approval from their fathers.

The costs boys must pay for complying with these messages— to separate, be tough, achieve, and *do* rather than *feel*—are very high. Men grow up experiencing, as Mick Jagger put it, "No satisfaction."[3] Boys are unlikely to find "satisfaction," a connection to themselves and to others that feels good, one that represents love, acceptance, and security, because we raise them to ignore or avoid emotions. They will cope with this in various ways.

Performance-oriented behaviors begin very early as a logical attempt to obtain contact and feedback from fathers, to lessen the pain of separation, and to get some "satisfaction." We see these tough little boys—playing on midget football teams, getting teeth knocked out, and ruining their knees. They push themselves to excel, imitating their fathers' behavior and hoping for their attention and a deeper connection. While most boys try to achieve, and in some cases, to live out father's fantasies, others will reject these values. Instead they will rebel, perhaps have trouble in school, or even engage in criminal activities. These boys develop a hard shell to cover up the loneliness and rejection. Still the underlying drive is the same: they crave satisfaction—a connection that feels good.

When boys leave childhood and enter adolescence without making satisfying attachments, they arrive wounded. They have learned to keep their feelings inside and to try to get their needs met in indirect ways. They have also accepted that men belong on the periphery of the family and are valued for accomplishments. Although they may have felt let down by their fathers, they also believe they should not need them. Many have heard how their fathers have sacrificed for them and do not feel entitled to ask for closeness; their fathers have given them their lives instead. A son's guilt about his needs soon is transformed into a subtle form of loyalty. This is evident in young men who attempt to resolve feelings of loss, anger, and guilt by adopting a lifestyle and values similar to their fathers'. Those who went through a period of rebellion may feel especially remorseful, and will cope by being excessively loyal.

The development of family loyalty is an unconscious, insidious, and powerful process[4] with the goal of finding some satisfaction, some connection. For example, young men whose fathers were absent from them because of career demands often become workaholics to create a bond with their fathers. Their father hunger is converted into accomplishments at work. They, like their dads, play a minimal role in their children's lives as they achieve in the world. On the other hand, men who do not succeed at work may become depressed and even abandon their families because of their inability to live out the allegiance they feel they owe their fathers and to follow the script that has been written for them. And the beat goes on: in an attempt to remain loyal to their fathers, men who were raised fatherless will raise their children the same way. Father hunger, perpetuated as loyalty to the old myths and traditions, remains unchallenged.

Some men cope with their need for connections through an exaggerated loyalty to father's values. For example, they may try to surpass their fathers economically. Those who accomplish this sometimes find, however, that by doing so they have abandoned the family's value system and are facing an unfamiliar high-pressure lifestyle. As these men confront adult experiences for which their fathers did not prepare them, they feel especially let down and neglected. They are workaholics who have no energy for personal relationships. They lack a connection with both their fathers and their families, with both the past and the present.

Some men are forging new ground by trying to be more emotionally involved with their families. Some are doing inner work. However, like their counterparts who are trying to surpass their fathers materially, they also may feel fatherless, abandoned, and ill-prepared.

Most men in our society, despite the variant paths they may take in their significant relationships, had absent, uninvolved fathers. They enter adulthood, marriage, and parenthood with serious wounds caused by a socialization process that has alienated them from their feelings. They are left with a deep despair and yearning for connection with their fathers. Having paid dearly for separation, they experience little or no satisfaction in relationships with themselves and with others, and are poorly equipped to parent their children, particularly adolescent daughters.

THE MASCULINE VALUE SYSTEM

The pressures on men to separate so completely result in a value system, world-view, and set of behaviors that are sex-specific and handicap fathers in their role within the family. The emphasis on separation allows men much power in the world. However, the same values and behaviors that engender status outside the family are often not appreciated at home. In fact, the actions and attitudes that assure men success at work often lead to disappointment in intimate relationships. This is a double-bind: fulfillment in the world too often leads to emptiness at home. Thus, the cycle of mutual father hunger continues: fathers are hungry for contact and appreciation and children hunger for their attention.

The values of self-control, independence, autonomy and individuality emerge from this emphasis on separation. They are further encouraged by a socialization process that teaches boys to need no one, to be in charge of themselves, and not to let others boss them around. They learn to assert themselves, protect their turf or reputation, and fight for their rights. The use of physical aggression or violence, if necessary, is acceptable. If a boy does not have the brawn or inclination to fight, he is considered inadequate, a "sissy," and will probably be socially ostracized. He is to seek freedom and autonomy and exude self-direction and power over himself and others.

In contrast to girls, boys learn to ignore the opinions of others. Consequently, their self-esteem and sense of personal identity will be less affected by the opinions of others than a girl's would be. While girls perceive popularity to be a measure of personal worth, boys stress independence, skills, competence, and achievement.[5] Boys will be less concerned about hurting other people's feelings and will take risks much more frequently as a result. Even if they are afraid to do something, males feel a push to "just do it" and not to worry so much about interpersonal consequences. The decision-making process is thus very different for the two sexes, with men making quicker, more purely rational choices and women constantly considering the implications for their relationships. So while "the moral imperative... with women is an injunction to care,"[6] for men it is to respect individual rights and independence.

These opposing values cause boys and girls to react differently to many of life's experiences. For example, if you watch children in a playground, you can see the impact of these divergent styles on their social behavior. You will probably notice that boys seem to enjoy active play more than girls do. (Could this behavior reflect the interactions that were encouraged for boys during feeding and eating? Remember that, right from the start, mothers tend to allow male infants more opportunities for active play during feeding, while they encourage female infants to be neat and tidy and to experience feeding in a less physical way. Because feeding times occur so often during the first year of life, the interactions that take place during them become ingrained and may well affect the child's play behaviors later.) You will probably also observe that boys' play lasts longer than girls' and that it is apt to continue even when there are misunderstandings. Boys tolerate disputes (maybe even enjoy them) and settle them so that the game can continue. If a controversy erupts when girls play, however, they are more likely to end the game or to change the rules rather than to risk causing animosity. In fact, fearing disagreements, girls will gravitate toward playing less competitive games. So, during play, boys are learning how to organize people and negotiate problems, while girls learn that it is more important to show caring for others and to avoid competition.[7]

With such divergent backgrounds, a father and a daughter will bring very different skills and attitudes to all their interactions with each other. Fathers will enjoy doing and accomplishing things, while daughters may just want to talk and share emotions. While men may emphasize the product, the principle, or the achievement, girls will value the process. Fathers may stress and reward competition, but daughters may be scared to achieve, not wanting to hurt anyone. Finally, while men value independence, their daughters may appear dependent because they crave connections. This discrepancy between masculine and feminine scripts and values causes much misunderstanding between men and women and certainly influences how the adult father and adolescent daughter negotiate their relationship. Men become fathers prepared to be separate, independent, and unemotional, while their daughters need to be connected, interdependent, and expressive. This creates father hunger.

BODY IMAGE, SEXUALITY, FOOD, AND NURTURANCE

The emphasis on separation also determines how men feel about their bodies, sexuality, food, and nurturance. As a result, their behavior in these areas is distinctively male, leaving them no experiential base from which to develop an intuitive understanding of what their daughters are feeling and experiencing.

This adult outcome arises from a process that starts very early in development, when boys and girls receive opposite messages about physical pleasure. Parents make unconscious decisions on issues as simple as clothing that may have a lasting impact on the bodily experience. They clothe male babies and toddlers in comfortable garments designed for activity and exploration. Boys are thus encouraged to have fun and not to be constrained by their clothing. They see their bodies as tools for pleasure and enjoyment—their own property, not mom's.

As they grow, boys often consider a bigger body an advantage because it will bring opportunities to pursue sports or other activities that require greater size or strength and will allow them to "perform." In fact, boys in preadolescence and adolescence often want to gain weight[8] to be like many of their heroes who are sports figures with large physiques. Sometimes men will engage in self-destructive activities such as steroid abuse, dietary changes, or excessive exercise to attain a bigger, more muscular body. Furthermore, a broad variety of male body types have been historically regarded as normal, so men are often able to accept their bodies.

The experience of sexuality is also sex-specific. Boys feel that their bodies will give them pleasure and often power, so they welcome getting bigger and stronger during puberty. While performance anxiety may be troublesome, males are less conflicted about sexual activity because they are more accepting of their physical shape, size, and impulses. Sex may be a release for men, but women tend to worry about it. They criticize their bodies, believe that men will never really like them, and obsess about pregnancy. Overall, whereas puberty, maturation, and sexuality raise conflicts and signify a loss of power and increased self-doubt for women, men associate these changes with enhanced status and prowess.

The impact of the aging process is also a different experience for men and women. While men are seen as more attractive and powerful as they grow older, women's beauty and influence decline because of the cultural values of western society. A birthday card a friend of mine sent to my husband is a perfect example of this contrast. On the cover is a cartoon drawing of a woman looking somewhat sad and a man smiling; it says: "Women get old. Men get distinguished. Women get wrinkled. Men get rugged. Women get senile. Men get charming." And inside it says, "I was going to wish you a happy birthday but I'm not sure if I like you anymore."[9]

Just as men experience their bodies as bringing them freedom, they view aging as ensuring control and power. In contrast, women experience both their bodies and the aging process as prisons. While men feel empowered as they grow older, women feel equally disempowered. Aging is not completely free of conflict for men. Some experience mid-life crises and anxiety when physical prowess begins to decline. In response, they may exercise excessively to stay fit or may become involved with younger women to prove their virility.

When a man is experiencing such conflicts, the relationship between father and daughter may suffer. His discomfort with himself and insecurity or impulsivity regarding sexuality may frighten her. If he seems preoccupied by sex or becomes more overt in his own sexual behaviors, she becomes confused, not knowing how to react because her needs for parental support and stability during her adolescence are so strong. In addition, the father's tendency toward separation and denial make him oblivious to his daughter's needs and reactions. The distance created results in the daughter's deepening sense of father hunger.

Men and women also may differ in how they relate to food. Men are more accepting of themselves physically and may feel freer to enjoy eating because they worry less about their weight. They receive few messages to change their bodies from advertisers in the diet and fashion industries. In contrast, women often see food as an enemy, something they must conquer. Also, since men experience other areas in which they feel in charge, controlling what they eat is not viewed as a measure of self-worth.

Moreover, men usually do not feel compelled to cook, since this duty generally falls on women. Again, their relationship to food, be it cooking or eating, can be one of pleasure. Similarly, nurturing others, through food or other caretaking behaviors, is an optional rather than required. On the other hand, many men avoid opportunities to cook or do other domestic tasks because they are afraid to fail. The strong achievement orientation they receive can create many obstacles to engaging in the parental behaviors that children find reassuring. They may never really know how to nurture or "feed" relationships.

The constant messages to achieve and to be autonomous can mask men's natural desire to connect with others. These patterns result in chronic intimacy problems for both sexes. Men feel disconnected from the father who was never there for them and consequently are unable to be there for their daughters. Since the daughter's relationship with her father will be the prototype for her relationships with all men, her father hunger will color the rest of her life. Both seek, but do not find, satisfaction.

Let's take a minute to summarize the problems in male development that may lead to later difficulties in close relationships such as parenting. Because of the way they are raised and the denial they are taught, men become cut off from their feelings and mechanical in their actions. They are not born this way but are created in this mold by our culture. As little boys move away from their mothers, they have no one to move toward. Their fathers are generally unavailable, so the pressure to separate from mom leaves little boys feeling alone and isolated. As they mature, they have difficulty getting close to other people, because past example has taught them that closeness eventually leads to abandonment. Since boys have few opportunities to seek nurturance from men, they do not see male relationships as being helpful or comforting. In the rare instances when we endorse closeness for men, such as the mentor for the young man, we convey that this is time-limited. In short, men are told that to develop, they must separate from the important people in their lives.

We constantly endorse this separateness and isolation. Consequently, when men become husbands and fathers, building a close relationship is not easy for them. Their script tells them to work and to support other people economically, but not to express or expect much from others emotionally. The developmental process as it unfolds in our culture creates adult men and fathers who are wounded, fearful of close relationships, and inept at feeling and expressing emotions. They cannot meet the needs of their adolescent daughters. Consequently, father hunger continues.

Questions and New Connections

• How has the pressure on men to be separate and independent affected the men in your life? How has it affected your relationship with them?

• Do you agree that most men grow up wanting more from their fathers? How has this been evident in your life? How has this affected your relationships either as a child or as a parent?

• Do you believe that your father was satisfied in his role as a parent? Did he feel connected to you? Adequate or inept? Close or distant?

• What do you know about his experience as a son? What was his relationship like with his father? Would he have changed it if he could?

CHAPTER 5

◆ ◆ ◆

THE DAUGHTER'S DILEMMA:
Female Psychological Development

In this chapter we shift our attention from how male psychological development creates father hunger to how female psychological development reflects it. Only recently has attention been given to the special problems for girls growing up in our culture. The "psychology of women" is a new, evolving body of knowledge with as many questions as answers. However, one certainty is that men and women are very different from each other. These discrepancies often create huge obstacles to father-daughter relationships.

Traditionally, much of the research in the field of psychology has been based upon a male model of development. Since the women's movement, however, feminists have challenged this and have gradually influenced research. Psychologists now realize that male-oriented theories stressing independence, separateness, autonomy, and individual rights cannot be used to describe women's modes of thinking and functioning. Men and women need to understand these disparities in order to create positive, mutually-fulfilling relationships.

Psychology's new appreciation of the differences between men and women will help us understand the origins of father hunger. In short, males are forced into separation and isolation, have problems with intimacy, and thus may not know how to father. Females are pressured to put others first, and have difficulty separating; thus, they need to feel connected and may not be satisfied by a peripheral father. The yearning to be close to dad and to feel part of his world leads many women to have severe problems with food and body image. While boys cope by over-achieving and performing, girls manipulate their eating and weight to deal with their uncertainty about their ability to succeed or survive in the masculine system outside the home.

Because they have learned to express themselves in such discrepant ways, fathers rarely understand the agony of their daughters' father hunger. Neither will find "satisfaction" in their relationship unless they understand the uniqueness of the male and female experiences. Articulating these differences will help both of them find common ground so that father hunger can eventually be satisfied.

THE MESSAGE TO WOMEN: CONNECT, CONNECT, CONNECT!

While separation is the constant theme as males develop, connections and relationships represent the equivalent mandates for women. Pleasing people supersedes satisfying oneself, because it promises the deeply-desired bond with others. Paradoxically, caring for others forms the center of the self for females. Men are encouraged to be independent and to focus on themselves, but females receive subtle and not so subtle messages that they should ignore their own needs and devote themselves to gratifying others.

According to Jean Baker Miller, who has written extensively on the psychology of women, "Women's sense of self becomes very much organized around being able to make and then maintain affiliation and relationships."[1] This tradition continues, because as little girls watch their mothers and identify with them, they learn not only that relationships and connections are very important to women, but also that taking care of others is central to their lives. Mothers make special efforts to teach little girls to take care of younger children and male family members, but rarely do they encourage their sons to act this way. Beginning very early in the socialization process, these other-directed behaviors become the female's way of ensuring attachments and connections.

Women easily adopt a pattern termed "otheration"[2] wherein they over-react to external demands and under-react to internal cues. As you may remember from the last chapter, mothers more frequently allow boys to set their own schedule, play with their food, and experience mealtime in a manner that suits their own impulses.[3] When they discourage their daughters' active play and experimentation with food, mothers begin to convey that little girls should control their appetites and look neat, clean, and tidy, thereby helping to make their environment look attractive. Starting early, the pressures on little girls endorse, maybe even require, that cooperation and attention to the desires of others be put above satisfying their own natural curiosity.

Fulfillment for males may mean pleasing the self and being autonomous, but for females it usually denotes satisfying everyone else. In fact, when girls as young as seven years old are asked to describe themselves, they give examples of how others have depicted them; boys report their own perceptions instead.[4] This otheration leads to many problems, particularly a lack of self-assertion in relationships and deficits in self-awareness. Extreme expressions of this common pattern are the eating problems and denial of the body's physical and nutritional needs that endanger many women today.

Since we emphasize relationships for girls, we also allow them much more closeness with mother than we do for boys. In adolescence, however, when they are expected to become more separate from the family, many girls find it difficult to do this without losing their most intimate attachment, to mother. Today, female teenagers experience additional pressure because cultural changes in women's roles require that they achieve outside of the traditional female realm. Their life experience may be very different from their mothers' and they may fear surpassing them and losing their approval by being more successful in school achievement or work accomplishments. Adolescence underlines the conflicts between the traditional caretaking values of femininity, and the achievement and performance expectations of the masculine world.

Facing these tensions and choices and feeling insecure with peers, girls may begin to associate the adolescent period with a loss of important relationships. This feeling is especially intense for girls whose fathers are not available to them at a time when they are feeling the pressure to be more separate from mom. A connection with father could assure them that future relationships have the potential for intimacy and caring, and that they will find a comfortable balance between dependence and independence and between femininity and masculinity.

THE COSTS OF CONNECTIONS: SELF–DENIAL, CONFUSION, GUILT, CODEPENDENCE

Just as the costs of separating are high for men, so are the costs of women's connections: self-denial can lead to identity confusion, guilt, and codependency, providing fertile ground for eating and body-image problems. Generally, however, we do not see these consequences until adolescence. Preadolescent girls assert strong opinions and often appear confident and self-assured. Carol Gilligan[5] describes this healthy resistance simply, "Eleven-year-olds are not for sale." They appear capable of balancing the needs of self and others fairly effectively.

Something changes, however, when girls move into adolescence. During this time, most girls have switched from confidence to confusion and from self-assertion to self-denial. Even though adolescent girls may appear competent, they rarely feel it. Instead, they are unsure and often ashamed of their thoughts, desires, and feelings. This transformation reflects some of the dilemmas we have regarding sex roles and values. Specifically, Gilligan attributes it to the feelings aroused in girls as they become more aware of the culture and the social structure around them. They see women as having little power and being told to "keep quiet" and to "say nothing." Girls who had been strong, opinionated, confident preadolescents all of a sudden seem uncertain of themselves. When asked a question they are apt to answer, "I don't know."

Adolescent girls are often unprepared to face the new pressures of a modern world that appears to value separation and autonomy. They have learned to suppress their needs, to take care of others, and to avoid initiating activities; especially ones that involve taking risks or asserting oneself. Thus, teenaged girls doubt themselves at this juncture, wondering if they can satisfy both the emotional needs of others and the new expectations for them to achieve. They may perceive that women's strengths—their attentive and caring attitude and their emphasis on building relationships—are required but not rewarded in our masculine culture. It's no wonder that by the time they enter adolescence, females are confused rather than confident. They find it difficult to articulate their feelings and assert themselves. The more uninvolved the father, the more gut-wrenching this developmental passage will be, because they are unsure both of themselves and of their fathers' feelings. Despite this insecurity, they must try to find a place in the male-oriented system outside the family.

The clash between masculine and feminine attitudes and values experienced by female adolescents results in identity confusion that can be sidestepped by a preoccupation with food or appearance. For example, as they pursue sports, math, science, or other traditionally male areas, girls may begin to wonder if they are losing some of their femininity and becoming too masculine. Some react to this by becoming overly attentive to other people, by dieting to get the perfect body, and by being meticulous about their appearance to assure that their femininity will not be lost. They risk their health and are alienated from their natural hunger in an attempt to conform. On the other hand, if they don't try to please everyone else, these young women are filled with guilt and increasingly confused about the priorities their own feelings and needs should have in the overall scheme of things. Regardless of their own desires, girls believe they should at least try to fulfill the world's expectations of them, even though they do not expect to succeed at this. Thus, the pattern of otheration that began in early childhood continues, but it runs at cross-purposes to the newer emphasis on the woman's individual development, resulting in chronic self-blame and remorse.

Guilt accompanies the female psyche the way isolation accompanies the male psyche. Men learn to ignore feelings and women obsess about how they caused the underlying problem. The development and advances of mass communication have only intensified this self-reproach and denial. Today, constant messages from the media bombard women of all ages. Growing girls are exposed to advice on how to raise children, please a man, keep the family healthy with good cooking, have a successful career and earn lots of money, and do all these things effortlessly while maintaining a perfect figure and a fashionable appearance! Judging themselves by impossible standards, they feel that "I'm never enough and perhaps I never will be." This provides fertile ground for female guilt to grow.

Expansion of the guilt quotient is probably closely associated with the yearning for a connection with their fathers and other men in their lives, and a worry that, whatever path they choose, they will not please them. Girls are more confused today about how to satisfy their dads because they have more options than ever before. They can pursue higher education, athletics, business, and other areas previously seen as masculine. Even though they may follow these interests primarily to satisfy their father hunger, they often still find the connection with dad tentative or inadequate. They blame themselves for this disconnection, believing that they alone are accountable.

Young women bring their self-blame and their longing for paternal approval to their marriages and other interactions with men. As adults, they try harder than ever to take care of their husbands and families and to be sure that their own activities or interests do not deprive the family. They constantly juggle roles and duties, hoping to satisfy others first, but usually experiencing the unpleasant effects of chronic guilt. Similarly, women who choose a single or lesbian lifestyle feel inadequate as well. In a male-dominated culture, a woman without a man receives many negative messages. Thus, it may be nearly impossible to feel good about the path she has taken.

Guilt can also overshadow the self-esteem and mental health many women experience when they work outside of the home.[6] Consequently, they will continue to place their husbands' or families' needs first, further ignoring their own. This is the result of years of otheration and explains why women easily become involved in codependent relationships. Codependency is a mechanism that helps one avoid facing problems directly in order to preserve some closeness in a family relationship. An example is the wife who, feeling guilty for pursuing her own career and taking time away from the family, excuses her husband's alcoholism. This woman may fear that her work distresses her husband and concludes that she should not complain about his drinking. If only she took better care of him, he wouldn't drink, or so she thinks. In this way, codependency is both a means of avoiding guilt and of maintaining connections.

Unfortunately, guilt about desires for personal growth, subordination of feelings, and excessive care-giving continue to be transmitted from mothers to daughters today. Girls learn their legacy early. Their chronic attempts to feel connected by satisfying others coupled with an over-developed sense of responsibility place them at great risk for problems with food, self-image, and relationships.

APPEARANCE AND IDENTITY: A SPECIAL CORRELATION FOR WOMEN

Appearance has a unique meaning for women, reflecting both their connections with themselves and with others. Women know they can please others through their bodies.[7] As a result of the increasing hunger for approval from men and the strict norms for female beauty, many women begin waging war with their bodies at extremely young ages.

Earlier, we discussed the powerful force of "otheration," a tendency to overvalue the opinions or needs of others and to undervalue one's own feelings. We also established that women feel it is important to make and maintain relationships. "Looking pretty" is a way to do this, a pursuit we begin instilling in little girls during infancy. For example, parents dress their female infants in pretty, detailed, matching outfits, which are often impractical and uncomfortable. Boys' clothes seem to say "have fun, move around" but girls' clothes seem to say "stay clean, don't do much." When girls are only infants, we teach them tidy eating to keep them pretty and clean; when they start school we encourage neat drawings and written work. We emphasize attention to detail and appearance over fun and learning. Furthermore, we begin the strange phenomenon of the beauty contest when they are as young as three or four years old. Similar to the adult version of these events, these little women must smile prettily, act coy, and be dressed in feminine, frilly outfits to win adult praise.

Girls learn these lessons well; they will spend countless hours and dollars during the rest of their lives in the pursuit of fashion and beauty. Ironically though, it is a losing battle, because although other cultures have recognized the grace and charm in maturity, ours does not. As women mature, they have to face the fact that their changes in appearance run counter to what our society endorses as being beautiful. Consequently, mothers who feel their own looks are declining may put special emphasis on their daughters' physical presentation.

This attention to female appearance is not new. It can be found throughout history, but today this pressure is more pervasive and culturally endorsed. What's more, their other-orientation makes girls easy targets for the advertisers of any fashion item or beauty product that promises acceptance or approval. Girls growing up in the United States are barraged by magazines and other media that present only the "perfect," "beautiful," thin female body and all kinds of unhealthy products to get it. Pick up any women's magazine (even those for preteens) or tune into any television program (even those for preschoolers). You will see pretty, thin, outwardly-successful and happy females advertising cosmetics, laxatives, diuretics, diet pills, liquid diets, exercise equipment, and even cosmetic surgery. All promise the "perfect" body that will please others and show how much the female consumer cares about her appearance.

The models we see in these ads have become increasingly thin over the past 30 years, establishing a standard of beauty that few can, or should, attain. But women will try hard to get that look because of their oversensitivity to what they perceive as the wishes of others. So, not only do advertisers use the woman's body to market consumer goods, but women themselves utilize their bodies as commodities to obtain power or acceptance in the world. Being thin and attractive represents a sure way to power for many women who are unsure of their abilities.

We can appreciate how easy it is for external factors to take hold when we realize how natural it is for a woman to scrutinize her body. Girls experience dramatic changes as they mature physically. In boys, the onset of puberty brings with it the growth of body and facial hair, a deeper voice, and a rush of hormones. But in girls it produces marked changes in the entire physical self. The flat breasts, undefined waist, and straight hips of childhood are replaced with curves and contours. Menstrual periods often cause severe cramping and discomfort as well as uneasiness and self-consciousness about the possibility of spotting through one's clothes. Every month, hormonal fluctuations cause ups and downs in mood, as well as changes such as bloating, facial pimples, and an increased desire for food, all of which bring a woman's attention back to her body. A woman's awareness and natural examination of physical changes associated with pregnancy, post-partum reaction, and menopause, make her an easy mark for the fashion and beauty industries throughout her life span. Because many advertisers have found ways to capitalize on the process of self-scrutiny in women, what were once natural processes have now grown to unnatural proportions.

When we consider the effects of normal body scrutiny combined with the pressures exerted on women by the beauty and fashion industries and the uncertainty today's women feel about their female identity, it is easy to understand why women are overly concerned about their appearance. Compared to men, women are more discriminating, more exacting, and more critical of their bodies. When a woman describes her shape, she is less accepting of its natural contours, her weight, and her overall image; often she will overestimate her size.[8]

Even before adolescence, a girl's perception of her weight affects her self-esteem. By fourth grade, girls strongly believe that being thin will bring popularity and social success. One writer describes women's self-scrutiny as a "devastatingly fierce, visual acuity" that "operates almost as a third eye."[9] And, while many women engage in self-scrutiny because they believe they must have a perfect body in order to please the opposite sex, men are probably far less critical of women's appearance than are women.

A woman can be her own worst enemy when she engages in excessive ruminations about what will satisfy men. (If only men and women would talk more together, women might be kinder to themselves!) Even when they are marketing "the natural look," the beauty and fashion industries have somehow convinced most people that men will only be attracted to thin women who are concerned with their appearance.

Men often have difficulty understanding why women expend so much energy and suffer so many inconveniences just to try to be fashionable. This brings us back to the differences in the socialization of males and females. Boys are encouraged to be independent and to take risks; girls are encouraged to be nurturant and to seek approval. By adolescence, females are steeped in a way of relating to others and to themselves that depends to a great extent on other-directed behaviors. Their self-knowledge is minimal but their desire to satisfy the world is maximal. Thus, girls tend to look at themselves through the eyes of others. Their self-image is dependent on what they believe people think of them. They are constantly comparing themselves to that pretty and thin female image portrayed in the media. The perceived contrast between these images and the reflections they see of themselves in the looking glass may be the most powerful contributors to a woman's self-image. As one recovered anorexic stated:

> When a man looks in the mirror, he can tell himself, "You may be an ugly old devil but you're brilliant, successful, virile." When a woman looks in the mirror she sees the totality of her being. Because of the social brainwashing to which she has been subjected, the mirror seems to tell her more than it can tell a man.[10]

Men often enjoy their bodies and see them as tools to bring pleasure, but women wage war with theirs, believing that they will finally receive the approval they need from their fathers or other men if they have the perfect body.

THE FEMININE CATCH-22:
COOKING AND DIETING

To understand why food is experienced so differently by men and women, we again need to ground ourselves historically. Anthropological studies show us that no matter what era or group is examined, women have borne the important responsibility of feeding others, just as they have had a near-monopoly on child care.[11] In many families today, men are learning to cook and trying to help in the kitchen. But their role is generally that of an assistant, not the person in charge. Primary responsibility for any task brings a deeper investment in the outcome of the activity, and along with it, a sense of burden. So men and women approach cooking with different purposes and emotions.

Little girls learn that food and meal preparation will become their responsibility when they grow up. They watch their mothers, aunts, and grandmothers face the daily kitchen chores and may observe that often women don't enjoy this activity. They may interpret this lack of pleasure as a forewarning of the central but sometimes negative role food will play in their lives. Today, even though many mothers are working outside the home, the responsibility for meals usually belongs to them. Food preparation and eating together as a family may have become less important and take less time because of the changes in our lifestyle and the availability of convenience foods. But, as we shall see, they still cause conflict. Food is one more factor that the two sexes experience quite differently and that contributes to the frequency of women's problems with eating.

Cooking causes more conflicts for women today than it ever has before. One reason is that food and its preparation have become more visible to us. New studies about nutrition contradict the old ones and confuse us about which foods are the right ones to give our families. Furthermore, a high level of technology has enabled the manufacture of many sophisticated devices for food preparation, and advertising incessantly announces their availability to us. Thus, meal preparation has become the newest field in which women must seek to be fashionably up-to-date.

Like the fashion world, the food industry constantly urges us to change our ways and try something different, new, and better. Women are particularly receptive to these messages because they believe that they are responsible for taking care of others and assuring the good health of their families. The media promote this by promising women that the right foods and their correct preparation will assure a family's well-being. Every week, television shows, commercials, newspapers, and magazines deluge us with claims about a new food that is declared to be an anti-cancer, anti-aging, or anti-cholesterol agent. Although the underlying research may be faulty, the news makes a good story or promotion. These reports can be perplexing to all of us. Because of women's desire to take care of others and their socially-ascribed role as the feeder of the family, they are more vulnerable to these suggestions and become more confused and conflicted than men do.

Their changing role in our society further complicates how women interpret these messages about food and cooking. As more and more women work outside the home, they feel increasingly guilty about being less than a fulltime homemaker. Taking care of their families' health and looking after their nutritional needs is a way of dealing with this guilt. Despite many changes and new responsibilities, women are holding on to the role of cook, probably as a way to assure continuity with the past and to retain a connection with traditional female behavior. Just as men often use sports or other physical activities to prove their masculinity and to gain approval, women show their femininity and their desire for relationships through cooking.

The dilemmas women experience regarding food are intensified by the pressures they receive to be thin. Although the way to a man's heart may be through his stomach, as tradition dictates, the way to get male attention is to be thin. In order to satisfy the need for connections with men, therefore, they have to feed them, but restrict their own intake. The diet industry, like food and fashion, aims its advertising and recruitment at women for whom dieting has become a normal activity. In fact, at any given moment, over 50% of adult women in the United States are trying to lose weight! It's no wonder that little girls believe that dieting is an essential part of being female—you might say that it is a rite of passage. Recent studies have found that by the age of 13, 80% of girls have attempted to lose weight (compared with only 10% of boys)[12] and that in some metropolitan areas where life is more fast-paced and children experience adult pressures earlier, up to 50% of nine-year-old girls and 80% of ten-year-old girls have already done so.[13]

Dieting is so well accepted, and even expected, that the amount of money spent on it nearly doubled between 1980 and 1990. In 1990 alone, Americans spent over 33 billion dollars on weight loss classes and products.[14] By the mid-1990s, income from the diet industry in the United States should exceed 50 billion dollars. This exceeds the annual projections for the entire federal Education, Training, Employment, and Social Services budget by 5-10 billion dollars for these years.[15]

Of course, most of this money is being spent by women. Their dilemma is: how can I feed my family but deny my own appetite so that I can be thin? Some women try to solve this conflict by preparing full dinners for their family while they heat frozen meals of less than 300 calories for themselves. Their daughters are watching this, previewing the struggles with food that they will probably inherit.

In the United States, food problems have no age limit. Older women worry about their weight and appearance almost as much as younger women. They see being thin as a way of looking youthful and attractive. Conflictual perceptions surrounding food can be traced back to the Garden of Eden, when Eve ate the forbidden apple in search of herself and a meaningful place in the world.[16] So, as women struggle with their eating, they are searching for meaning, identity, and a "place."

If we remember how important it is for women to please others and to have satisfying relationships, it is easier to understand why women are so susceptible to the advertising campaigns and images in the media about who they "should" be. As they face dramatic changes in their roles and become bewildered about their place in the world, a retreat to developing the perfect body may be appealing, especially for young women. They are searching for themselves, but do not have an internal structure that is strong enough to help them resist the conflicting messages they receive, and to be objective about the pressures they are under. The unrelenting struggle will be translated into conflicts with food and with their feminine bodies.

Daughters bring a very different psychological history and sense of self to the relationship with their fathers. Until recently we have ignored this, but now we have enough information to help us understand the origins and ongoing contributions to the daughter's father hunger. Because each one is raised with disparate demands and expectations, a father does not understand his daughter's need for close, intimate, emotionally-disclosive interactions and her equally strong drive to please others. Nor do fathers comprehend the emotions and conflicts women experience surrounding their bodies, weight, appearance, and food. Men have found power and satisfaction through larger, stronger, active bodies, but their daughters usually see approval and status coming from diminished size and through cosmetic assistance. Fathers rarely understand how the media and its images of thin women impact their daughters because they were raised not to be influenced by outside sources; they were constantly told to be independent and to make their own decisions. These differences feed father hunger.

As the role of women has changed in western society, fathers are even more important to their growing daughters, and father hunger has greater risks. One of the dilemmas daughters face is how to balance pressures to achieve and be autonomous in a masculine world with their feminine needs to nurture and please others. Women have not yet mastered how to care both for oneself and for others without feeling guilt. Girls need help and guidance from both parents to know how to surmount these problems and forge a personal identity. Although girls need their fathers to help them understand masculinity and femininity so they can negotiate a balance between the needs of others and their own needs, most will experience father deprivation rather than father contact.

They will choose physical hunger by dieting or abusing their bodies, desperately hoping for his attention rather than face the pain of his neglect. They will bring this father hunger to all their other relationships as they seek approval, acceptance, and love.

Questions and New Connections

• How has the pressure to connect affected you and other women in your life?

• Do you agree that most girls want more of a relationship with their fathers? How has this been evident in your life?

• What are the most difficult issues females face as they grow up? How can their fathers help them with these?

• How do men and women differ in their relationship to food and their bodies? How does that affect their relationships with themselves and each other?

PART TWO

◆ ◆ ◆

THE EXPERIENCE OF FATHER HUNGER

CHAPTER 6

◆ ◆ ◆

DAMAGE TO A DAUGHTER'S EMOTIONS AND IDENTITY

The central problem in the father-daughter relationship is the discrepancy between what daughters need and what fathers are equipped to provide. Daughters, with their deep need for connections and intimacy, will hunger for their dads who, valuing separateness and independence, will remain distant. This opposition leads to conflicting definitions of personal power, identity, self-direction, pleasure, self-esteem, affective expression, communication, goals, and values. As a result, fathers and daughters rarely understand each other.

These next chapters move from the theoretical and historical basis of father hunger to the feelings that result. The emotional consequences of father hunger become apparent as daughters approach adolescence and their need for contact and love from their fathers intensifies. When girls don't know their dads or don't feel valued by them, moving out of the family and becoming part of the culture where men have most of the power is not very enticing. Left unsatisfied, father hunger becomes converted into problems with food, body-image, self-esteem, and relationships. In this chapter, we will look at issues central to women's emotional development illustrated by the words and life stories of some who have suffered from eating disorders and from the damaging and long-term effects of not getting enough attention from dad.

EMOTIONAL CONNECTEDNESS

A woman needs to feel connected to others. Beginning very early in her development and continuing throughout her life, her sense of self, identity, and satisfaction are derived from relationships. In fact, emotional connectedness is usually her strongest drive, so taking care of others can easily become more important than taking care of the self.

At adolescence, when identity is forming and consolidating, relationships are particularly critical, and a young woman's interests naturally turn toward men at this time. The father, whose upbringing diminishes the importance of interpersonal connections and whose sense of self emanates from separateness, may not recognize these needs. The daughter begins to feel ashamed of her desire for contact with dad, assuming that something is wrong with her for wanting more from him. She may begin to doubt the validity of her appetites, be it for relationships, for food, or for sex. Surrounded by a culture and myths that convey that girls need only mothers and that fathers are a luxury, an adolescent female will do her best to deny her need for dad. Furthermore, convinced that she is unworthy of his affection, she may punish herself by not eating, overeating, purging, or over exercising. Thus, instead of acknowledging and mourning the loss of the desired connection to dad, she blames herself for her father hunger.

Even though I had a close relationship with my dad, I still was strongly influenced by cultural norms and underestimated the importance of this emotional connection. It took me a long time to realize how essential he was to my development and how significant the fathers of my patients are to them. Once I learned how to listen, I discovered that most adolescent and adult women suffer from their father's emotional distance and lack of involvement in the family's life. In their words, dad was "self-absorbed," "unavailable," "tied up in his own ego," and "incapable of dealing with feelings."

A father's inability to connect with his daughter causes her feelings of rejection, abandonment, self-doubt, anxiety, fear, and sadness. Many women in recovery see this relationship as one of the most significant contributions to their eating problems. The fathers' disengaged emotional style undermines young women in many ways, the most important of which is that their daughters never feel loved. When Liz (whose story you will read later) described what led to her anorexia, she said quite simply, "All I wanted was my father's love." What she craved and needed was an emotional connection to her father.

UNREQUITED LOVE

Women who struggle with eating and body-image problems often speak of unrequited love when they speak of their fathers. "I never felt good enough for him," is a common refrain. Many report having felt their fathers' disappointment throughout their entire lives. A chronic perception of unrequited love can be especially damaging to girls, since they attach earlier and more intensely than do boys.[1]

In most families with eating disorders, the fathers are good providers. In fact, they often take their traditional role as the economic head of the household so seriously that they have nothing left for the family. In the few cases I have known where the fathers were not described as good providers, more often than not these men had illnesses or suffered from depression. It is likely that in these cases, the fathers' low self-esteem was related to their inability to provide, which made it difficult for them to give their daughters love and affection.

Some women who develop eating disorders in response to this interpersonal background believe that their fathers' disappointment began at birth when they were born female instead of male. As one woman said:

> My parents had always wanted a boy. I was their last try. My father would tell me how disappointed he was. I felt close to him when I was little but it was very traumatic for me when I realized there was no relationship there. It crushed me. I realized I would never meet his expectations.

Sensing father's preference for sons and discomfort with daughters, many young women act out their father hunger by pursuing sports, academic achievement, or other interests of their fathers. Some begin by exercising excessively, often with their dads, and by pushing their bodies to the point of exhaustion. They will strive for a hard, lean body, believing that their dads will accept them if they achieve this. Often they pursue sports hoping to please their fathers rather than to fulfill any personal desires of their own. Like little boys, they convince themselves that if their performance is good enough, they will win dad's love.

While some daughters may pursue more masculine activities and be "tom-boys," others will try to exaggerate their femininity in response to their unrequited love. They attempt to sculpt their bodies through dieting, exercising, taking pills such as laxatives, diuretics, or appetite suppressants. Some may even have plastic surgery; still others may undereat to punish themselves or will eat uncontrollably to avoid the painful realization of the unrequited love they maintain for their fathers. All are endangering their health—even risking their lives—for love.

RUNNING ON EMPTY

Both fathers and daughters in the traditional western family feel the unrequited love we just discussed. Fathers, indoctrinated to believe that economic support of the family is their most important duty, bear many burdens for which they feel unappreciated. They come home at the end of the day, worried about work and money, with little energy left for the family. They "gave at the office" and are emotionally spent. An exhausted, depleted father has little to give. Negativity and resentment may fill the air, further validating the daughter's feeling that she is not loved. One woman summed it up with these words: "My father was always involved in his business and he was never affectionate. When he was there, he was just negative and critical."

An atmosphere of stress, fatigue, unhappiness, and disapproval does not create the secure home-life that young people need. Adolescence brings with it tremendous insecurity. Its passengers need to feel comforted, accepted, and loved at home to survive these turbulent tides. Teenaged daughters need to be emotionally supported and refueled by their fathers, since men's opinions are so central to them. Accepting the many changes associated with adolescence, particularly sexuality, is not just an internal process. Girls rely on others, especially their fathers, to help them integrate sexual maturity into their personal identities and lifestyles. When fathers are depleted, they have nothing to give their daughters. Both are running on empty.

CONSTRICTED COMMUNICATION

Communication problems and deficits in self–assertion also reflect basic differences between what each sex learns to value. For example, females want to know what others think and feel and bring this intense need to their fathers during adolescence as they try to understand and negotiate their position with the opposite sex. Males, however, have been taught not to show or verbalize their feelings, and so denial and control will be the skills a father brings to the relationship with his daughter. Usually fathers, who have internalized the economic-provider role the most will be the least proficient at personal communication. The result of keeping a lid on feelings inside, however, is outbursts of anger that can be very frightening to a daughter who so wants to please her father. As one woman described: "I was afraid of dad. He never talked much but he got angry easily. I guess he shut off all his feelings because of his temper."

The myth that men do not feel has devastating effects on young people who are learning how to communicate. Perceiving that emotions are off-limits, they will discuss the bare essentials but will ignore deeper issues. This communication pattern is like shorthand or some other special code—it expresses external, not internal, reality. This can be confusing and limiting to children.

Constricted communication is a communicable disease—it spreads easily. So although the father in a family may have the worst case, everyone else may also suffer. For example, one young woman whose father was unable to talk about feelings finally expressed her pain through her weight loss.

> My father had arthritis. I knew he was miserable but he would never talk about it. I felt so guilty whenever I complained because he never did. I think I'm a lot like my dad—I have a hard time talking about how I feel. Maybe that's why I had anorexia.

Many girls grow up not knowing how their fathers feel about anything and begin to doubt the validity of their own impulses and needs. "If dad doesn't have any feelings, should I?" becomes an underlying question, and they may try out the denial system their dads have modeled so well. Lacking the avenues for direct communication with her father, a girl will then use her body to say what she means.

PLEASING OTHERS

One of the damaging effects of constricted communication between fathers and daughters is that even basic messages of acceptance are absent. The result is that daughters grow up wondering how their dads feel about them, but they have no way of knowing since they never receive any feedback. They are quick to conclude that they have not "measured up" in some basic ways. They are desperate to please but don't know how.

Some daughters will cope with this need to please or satisfy their dads by trying to be like them. After all, imitation is the highest form of flattery! For example, one woman who recovered from anorexia described her father this way:

> Dad would never get into feelings with us. He did things for us but didn't talk. I used to fear him. He expected a lot from us and had a hot temper. He had no use for people who didn't carry their weight. So I was always on the go–go–go. I never wanted to be a slacker. I wanted to please him, but he never seemed to notice.

Trying to please her father, this woman rejected her body's needs and even stopped eating so she would not be seen as a "slacker." She and many other women who develop eating problems describe childhoods in which they would do anything to satisfy their dads, whom they often saw as overburdened and unhappy. Here's an example of the results:

> When I was six years old my father told me I was too old to play with dolls. I never did again. I couldn't play. To gain acceptance from him, I had to act mature instead. I tried hard to win his approval. It may be why I became a lawyer. The only way to get his attention was to do something drastic. My weight loss was the only thing that ever worked in getting his concern. But then he was as angry as he was worried.

Such experiences lead women to *expect* non-gratifying, critical, negative interactions with men. The die has been cast, and they may go through life often attracted to men who are just like their fathers, hoping sooner or later to please either daddy or his substitute. In this way, father hunger assumes a powerful position in a young woman's life. It creates a blueprint for future relationships with men and with a masculine culture, which creates a willingness to do anything to get male approval. One woman described this as follows:

> My father never talked to us much. I never knew how he was really feeling. . . I never got feedback about how I was. It would have helped if he had talked to me more. Recently I've been talking about him in therapy. I'm realizing that his ignoring me had an effect. I wanted his approval and probably have tried to get it from other men, not in a healthy way.

POWER

A healthy personal identity requires that we feel a sense of mastery and independence in the world. This, however, is a tricky process for women, since pleasing others is also necessary to self-identity. Many women are at a loss over how to assume power in a culture that rewards masculine characteristics more than feminine ones, where independence, autonomy, control, achievement, and economic productivity are valued more than nurturance and relationships. As young women today struggle to balance femininity and masculinity, they find it difficult to meet their own needs, to continue to please others, and also to assume a desired, possibly influential place in the world. They may also find that although self-assertion brings with it a sense of power and connection to those masculine values, it may jeopardize their relationships.

Girls who grow up feeling loved and respected by their fathers generate a sense of personal power which enables them to make and stand by decisions that balance the needs of the self with the demands of others. Those who don't enjoy this kind of connection will not easily achieve this equilibrium. One young woman described the impact of her father's absence on her inability to assert herself in relationships in this way:

I don't have any childhood memories of him. He's quiet. I don't remember him saying, "I love you," until I was 17. . . . If I had known him and if he had been an example for me, he could taught me that all men are not lechers and bastards. I had many experiences with that kind of man. I felt powerless as a woman and didn't know how to gain control of my life.

If my father had been there for me, he could have shown me that I'm not less than a man, that a woman can have her own ambitions, desires, needs, and can say what she needs.

A more open and accepting relationship with her father might have empowered this woman to make decisions, assert herself, and feel effective as a woman. Instead, she denied her femininity and withdrew from relationships. Not eating and losing weight became the one area in which she felt permission to exert her own personal power.

CONTROL

Food and control go hand in hand. Giving or withholding basic sustenance is a family's easiest and most frequent method of behavior modification. Parents constantly use it to reward, punish, or alter a child's behavior. So, quite naturally, children may engage in battles over food in order to gain some influence in their families. People who develop significant eating problems see changing their nutritional intake as their only way to exert autonomy. For example, one young woman whose parents had been very authoritative in all their interactions, including meals, described how eating became her sole means of control.

I was fed up with everything, sick of having to answer to everyone and follow what they wanted. I had always pleased my parents by being a good eater . . . My mother liked to cook and I always thought I was pleasing her when I ate . . . . And mealtimes were very important in my home. I started to feel that I had no power in the world—even eating was for others, not for me. I had to find something that was mine. I learned that I could control what I ate, how much—that's all I had, the only thing that was mine. So I used food to subvert my parents' control over me.

Although this young woman felt more pressure from her mother to conform to certain eating habits, she felt dominated and unappreciated by both parents. She expressed a desire to gain more control of her life through food, because mealtime was her only access to her father. She wanted him to hear her. Eating and not eating was a plea for father to respond to her as a person rather than just to dictate to her.

Excessive constraint over eating, however, soon leads the person to being tyrannized in a new way: now, worries about food, calories, fat, exercise, and ways to avoid eating or to get thin dictate every waking moment and interaction. As the same woman says:

> The ironic thing is that I only wanted control, and for a while I guess I had it. But before long, my life was totally out of control. First I was anorexic, then bulimic. I had to be hospitalized three times. I was sick for about four years. If only I had known how to gain real control in my life. I was really asking for my father to help me with this.

For many women, denying their need for food is an effort to reject their femininity and to curb their appetites for connections with others. By taming their hunger for food they hope they will also tame their hunger for daddy, for love, and for acceptance from men. Such constraint may be an attempt not only to follow the male pattern of being less connected to food, but also to make their bodies more masculine. Eating problems thus symbolize a different way of connecting with dad—through control.

ACHIEVEMENT

Girls learn early that men value achievement, so they search for ways to succeed in order to get dad's approval. One accomplishment highly valued by western society is a well-toned, slim, "perfect" body. The food, fashion, diet, and fitness industries constantly remind us that changing our food intake and our body shape will bring personal happiness and acceptance from others. As one woman said:

> I really wanted, needed, my dad to be proud of me. I wasn't sure how to get that—nothing I did seemed to work, but I knew he thought being thin was good, so I started to diet. It was the beginning of an eating disorder—but all I wanted was to please my dad. This was my only way to achieve. It showed self-control and all the things I thought he valued. But in the process, I nearly ruined my body and could have lost the basis of being a woman: being able to have kids. I didn't realize all that back then. I only knew I needed a way to achieve—I needed to be outstanding to feel O.K., to get approval from my dad.

Today we tend to define achievement in masculine terms. Objective measures, especially numbers—like how much money a person makes, how much a person weighs—determine an individual's worth to society. Competing and winning are considered accomplishments, while nurturing and caring are not. Consequently, to attain some sense of accomplishment, many young women will abuse their bodies attempting to win in an unspoken, society-wide beauty contest.

ATTENTION

As you have read, women who grow up without a positive connection to their fathers suffer tremendously from father's lack of attention. At no time do they experience that basic essential: knowing that they have satisfied their dad's needs, demands, and expectations. Since they have never received positive responses or approval from this most important man, they feel unworthy and undeserving of it. Some will become stuck in this web of father hunger and will be unable to go forward in their lives. Developing an eating disorder may represent their only chance of connecting with their fathers and getting the attention that all children need in order to grow.

Looking back at their eating problems, many women have told me that meals were the only times they saw their dads on a regular basis, so this was the logical time to try to get attention. If dad notices, then the eating problem is successful. Therefore, changing these behaviors and recovering may be a frightening prospect: what if they lose what they're worked so hard to attain? As one woman said,

> Finally my father came into my life a bit when I started to lose weight. That kept it going. I knew that I needed him and I had done a lot of other things, good and bad, to get it, but this was the only thing that worked and I was reluctant to stop.

Men simply do not know how important they are to their daughters' self-esteem. The gap between the attention most fathers give and what their daughters need has tremendous implications. Girls who hunger for their dads to notice them are bound to have a shaky sense of self as they enter adolescence and adulthood. If they do not feel acknowledged by dad, they will wonder how they can become part of the world he represents.

IDENTITY

The whole notion of female identity—what it is to be a woman—is in flux today. Young women are expected and encouraged to do many things they could never consider doing 25 years ago. As a result, women of all ages are bewildered as they consider which roles they should assume, what they should be like, what interests they can pursue, and how to balance what they know they must do (take care of others) with the new expectations that they achieve and be independent. Finding one's personal identity, a sense of a unified self and social role, is a great challenge to young people growing up in this period of change.

Our families shape our identities by both their actions and their attitudes. Parents today are struggling with old roles and definitions of masculinity and femininity that no longer fit and that confuse their daughters, who are trying to consolidate their sense of self and find a way to live in today's society. Jessica, who developed a serious eating disorder as a teenager, talked about the conflicting pressures she felt as she struggled with her female identity:

> In the world I grew up in, women were second-class citizens. I was tuned into that. I got angry with what my mother took. I think that's still lurking back there. I was getting double messages. I felt a need to achieve and I knew I was smart but I had iron shackles on my feet at the same time. I was getting the masculine push to achieve and the feminine go-to college-so-you-can-raise-better-children. That's still going on—the only time my father said he was proud of me was when I had my son. Anybody can have a kid!

Like many other young women today, Jessica was ambivalent and confused about growing up and preparing for the future: should she achieve or should she just prepare to be a good wife? She knew she did not want a life like her mother's, one that had been full of self-sacrifice, while "holding my dad on a pedestal." When she looked at her family and the surrounding culture, she did not anticipate finding a comfortable role as a woman.

Gradually, Jessica solved her dilemma about her feminine identity. Recognizing what she did not want was a big step for her, but that was followed by much turmoil. As an adult she reached a compromise between the two positions—she is now a wife and mother, works part-time, and feels quite fulfilled. Like many of her peers, she unfortunately battled her body and her appetites for food and relationships before she figured out how to "be" as a young woman.

For Jessica, an important part of finding her own path in adulthood was to understand the impact of the culture on her perceptions and on her family's functioning. She has concluded that the culturally-prescribed limitations on the father's role caused many of her problems. She now knows that her father's noninvolvement was not necessarily an active choice. Instead, it was prescribed by the social patterns at that time.

Jessica also determined that her childhood, adolescence, and identity formation may have been different if her father had been more involved with the family. If her parents had been able to work together more effectively, she might have grown up with clearer, more constructive views about being a women. A father's attitude and behavior toward his wife has a significant impact on his daughter's emerging female identity. For example, when her father belittled her mother and did not support her in the family, Jessica responded to this perceived lack of respect by trying to be different from her mother. She had no other model, however, so she became very confused about femininity and adulthood. Regrettably, like many other women, Jessica attempted to answer the questions about who she is, where she is going, and what place she has in the world, by changing her eating and her body. She thought that losing weight would bring her approval and power from a masculine culture.

An eating disorder can function as a developmental passage from childhood to adulthood, a way to forge a personal identity. By slowing down the process, it allows the person to avoid or delay facing the issues of adolescence and young adulthood. One young woman I met said she could not imagine how she would have become an adult woman without her eating disorder. In her words:

> The anorexia is part of becoming who you are. It's like being in a cocoon, building a wall around you for a while. Finally I could understand why I did it and feel O.K. about that.

For many young women suffering from father hunger, conflicts with their bodies and food become their protective cocoon. Just as a caterpillar breaks out of the cocoon as a butterfly, those who are fortunate will be transformed by the experience. This metamorphosis often includes a heightened awareness of their father's influence in their lives. This is apparent in the case studies that follow.

LIZ: "All I wanted was my father's love."

Liz's story illustrates many of the themes we have discussed in this chapter, especially the longing for dad's attention. It also challenges many of the myths we discussed earlier. Remember the quote earlier in this chapter, "All I wanted was my father's love."? Those were Liz's words. Her childhood memories speak to the importance of the father in the family, especially to his daughters.

Liz was the youngest of three girls. They all knew that their father wanted sons. She "went all out to be the son," playing softball, soccer, "but it was never enough." Being the youngest in the family put her in a difficult position. Not only did Liz feel she was her father's last chance for a son, but also she was young and the only child still at home when her parents divorced.

The family environment included many stressors that converged in an eating disorder for Liz. Her mother was weight-conscious; her father was achievement-oriented. He was a physician, devoted to his practice and profession, who did not leave much time for his wife or family. Liz felt that her mother expressed anger with her father by not cooking. They never even ate meals together! But, because her parents had lived like that for a long time and had not been fighting, her mother's matter-of-fact announcement that she was getting divorced really surprised Liz. Then her home life began to change. Her sisters left for college and until the divorce was final, her parents still lived together but they fought a lot.

Liz felt no one cared about her. Her sisters had left, her father was more preoccupied and distant than ever, and her mother was tense, angry, and began drinking. Her mother had never appeared happy as a homemaker and had not put much effort into providing meals or nurturing her daughters, but now she became even less involved. After her parents' divorce, Liz had less contact and time with her father and her doubts about his love for her grew. She wanted desperately to please him, so she pursued academics and athletics. She tried to be more like a boy, but nothing worked; nothing evoked her father's affection.

Liz's adolescence was miserable. From the age of 12, when her parents decided to divorce, she had problems in school. One year she nearly failed. Later she began smoking marijuana and drinking, leaving evidence in both of her parents' homes. They never responded to these behaviors, so Liz assumed they didn't care. They didn't seem to realize that she felt isolated, sad, and lonely. At her request, she went away to boarding school. Both of her parents remarried, and her mom spent a great deal of time with her new husband. Her father remained over-involved in his work.

Her eating problems began at age 20 while she was away at college. She had become engaged to a man who was much older than she. She questions now whether he was a replacement for her father. Their engagement and wedding plans brought her closer to her parents, but Liz soon realized she did not feel ready for a long-term commitment and broke up with her fiancé. Sadly, she felt she had also lost the new relationship she was beginning to build with her parents. Because she had always tried to be "the best" and "the strongest," she could not let her guard down and tell her parents she needed their help.

Until this time, Liz had not dieted or been unhappy with her body, although her roommate and many of the young women on campus seemed to be. After the break-up with her boyfriend, however she needed something to take his place, so she started to diet. Her father had always stressed the need to have a goal and a plan, and suddenly weight loss became her life's purpose. She said:

> I was so weak and vulnerable. I had no one. I had nothing else to do but to compete with my roommate in dieting and exercise. I was always striving to be perfect, to please my parents. When I realized that would never happen, I just stopped eating. I wanted just to slowly, passively waste away and not bother anyone.

Before she began dieting, she was 5'4" and weighed 120 pounds. Then she lost 35 pounds. Her father (remember, he was a physician) never mentioned her weight loss. Her mother never talked about it either, but did try to get her to eat. Liz did not find her mother's attempts helpful. Her stepmother appeared aware but didn't say anything until one day when she told Liz that her father was concerned and offered to go to therapy with her. Both her mother and stepmother tried to support her in their own ways, but Liz really wanted her dad's attention. As she said: "I was looking for my dad. That's all I wanted. I wanted something from *him*."

Gradually, with her stepmother's help, Liz realized that her father's inability to show affection did not mean he didn't love her. Although she never took advantage of their offers to attend family therapy with her, their willingness to do so helped her, and she began to accept her father's love through her stepmother.

Liz had been seeing a therapist and she continued to do so, although her recovery process continued long after she had stopped regular sessions. As she spoke about the importance of her sessions with him and his gentle, accepting support of her, I began to believe that a male therapist was especially appropriate for her.

Through this therapeutic relationship, Liz found that men can pay attention to feelings, can show caring and nurturance, can listen and be available, and can understand her complex problems. Although her father's behavior supported the myths about men being unable to care, feel, or understand; her therapist's behavior challenged them. Gradually she began to open up to men and to anticipate that they might understand. Liz found that, although initially difficult, developing a relationship of trust with a male therapist was reaffirming.

During her recovery, Liz felt she was becoming closer to her father, but she went through a long "anti-male phase" when she did not want to be alone with him. Gradually she developed friendships with men. She went on to finish college, then graduate school, and began a professional career. She is now married and has her own family. Liz and many other women have repeated the belief that "if only dad had been there, maybe this all would not have happened." They speak to the long-term and painful impact of father hunger.

PATRICIA: "I never felt that I was enough."

Patricia, who is now in her 40s and has a rewarding marriage, career, and three children, developed anorexia when she was a teenager. She feels her eating disorder was directly related to her father, who was a diabetic and became severely depressed. Patricia was an only child and a bright little girl who was very talented in music. She perceived that there was great pressure on her to achieve and to make up for her father's disappointments, "Because I did well, I think I created expectations in him that I would excel. My father felt he was a failure. I think he looked to me to fill some of his own hopes. I never felt that I was enough."

Patricia did anything she could to try to make her father happy. She began cooking for him as soon as she was old enough, even paying attention to his special dietary needs as a diabetic, but mealtimes were tense and unpleasant. Her parents argued when her father did not eat properly. Patricia had always been a picky eater herself and having to think about her father's dietary problems might also have contributed to her using food to help her cope with growing up. As her father became more depressed and withdrawn, her mother became increasingly angry. Patricia, who desperately wanted to please both of them and get their minds off their problems, became an overachiever:

> By the age of 15, I was a workaholic. I used to stay up till 2 or 3 A.M. doing homework. I felt there was no room for failure. I had to make up for their disappointments. I had to make up for my dad's depression and feelings of failure, but there was no room for failure for me. I remember I failed a test in driver education. My father was so angry—he called his friends demanding another test, but I refused to take it. I could have really used help with failing. I couldn't fail. Anorexia was another achievement and at the same time it was a way of rebelling against my father's demands.

Patricia had suffered from anorexia nervosa for seven years. She sees it as a response to her perceptions of what her family expected of her:

> There was a demand to be beyond my years, to make up for my dad's failures and their unhappiness. For me, I think I finally rejected that responsibility so I wouldn't become independent. I think I was saying "I'm not grown up enough to handle this."

Despite her weight loss (Patricia was 5'5" and got down to 75 pounds when she was sick), her parents could not face up to her problems. Although her mother would try to get her to eat, they never talked about why she wasn't eating. Patricia knows her father was concerned and remembers "seeing tears in his eyes," but he was discouraged and worried about himself. Her parents took her to their medical doctor who encouraged her to gain weight, but nothing really changed until after she went to college.

If Patricia's high school teachers worried about her weight loss, they didn't mention it, and as Patricia continued to achieve in school, they most likely discounted their worries. When a youngster seems so competent, so perfect, and so able to take care of others, adults may not recognize the emotional needs and deficits underlying this veneer. No one knew how much Patricia was suffering and how her father's illness, problems, and special needs were impacting her relationships, identity, and self-concept. She was sick, preoccupied, and isolated throughout high school, and her eating disorder worsened.

As a freshman in a prestigious women's college, Patricia continued eating very little and losing weight. Still, no one tried to find out why this was happening and no one referred her for therapy. Remember, Patricia was in college 20 years ago. Hopefully, if her situation happened today, it would be handled differently. Now most colleges have counseling and health services that can help students identify their problems and begin to work on recovery.

Late in her freshman year, the dean of the college took notice of her wasted body told her that if she continued to lose weight they would hospitalize her. By this time Patricia had internalized her father's expectations for her, and the threat of not being able to continue her pattern of achievement was frightening. Paradoxically, the same fear of failure that contributed to her eating disorder helped her to begin to gain control of her symptoms. She didn't want to disappoint her dad or anyone else. The dean's words shook her up and she slowly began to give her body what it needed.

In addition to regaining weight and her health, Patricia worked very hard to correct the patterns in her relationships that led her to focus on others rather than on herself. Gradually she learned how to develop relationships with men that were not completely based on self-sacrifice and otheration. As a result, she has developed many satisfying connections, including her marriage. Although it took three years for Patricia to gain weight and to begin menstruating again, she has recovered both physically and psychologically. However, she still wishes she could have experienced a better relationship with her now deceased father and mourns this loss and the loss of her adolescence. She sees her eating disorder as causing her years of misery, self-doubt, isolation, and poor health. Although she has been able to overcome these problems, her father hunger had costly consequences and could have destroyed her. To heal, she had to admit the sadness she experienced in her relationship with her dad and acknowledge its effects on her life.

CHAPTER 7

♦ ♦ ♦

CONFLICTS SURROUNDING SEXUALITY, BODY-IMAGE, AND FOOD

Fathers are a significant influence on their daughters' acceptance or rejection of sexuality, body-image, and eating and health habits. Still, old myths that ignore the fathers' contributions to these areas continue to flourish. By default, not by intention, fathers do not support their daughters' passage through adolescence to sexual maturity.

Part of the problem is that the two sexes experience life so differently. For example, because we teach men to fear, distrust, and deny feelings, we give them few opportunities to be emotionally open to others. Consequently, for many men, sex is the only time they feel permission to be close. So as the typical father watches his daughter mature and become increasingly sexual, he may be worried about boundaries and withdraw from her even more. Dad's anxiety combines with the daughter's own fear of her body's changes to become a powerful deterrent to their relationship and to her sense of herself as a budding young woman. The result can be a denial not only of sexuality but of all of her body's needs. This is apparent in anorexia, exercise abuse, bulimia, compulsive eating, and body-dissatisfaction.

FATHER HUNGER AND SEXUALITY

Father hunger becomes increasingly detrimental when girls enter puberty, because this is the developmental phase, when their curiosity about men and the male perspective, their interest in heterosexual relationships, and their own physical attractiveness emerge and intensify. When fathers withdraw or act aloof, their daughters suffer from low self-esteem and little confidence in their sexuality. They have no experience or practical knowledge in how to act around men or how to talk to them.

For many, dieting is a response, an effort to please men, to be sexually attractive, or to get attention. For others, the same behavior may be an effort to deny their physical maturity. As one woman who developed eating problems as an adolescent said: "In the back of my mind I was trying to have a body that wouldn't attract men and then I wouldn't have to worry." By reverting to a more juvenile body, she hoped to regress to her childhood, when relationships with her father and other men were unencumbered by sexuality.

Some women with eating problems report having been close to their fathers during childhood, but having felt abandoned or rejected by them as they matured. Most likely these men retreated or withdrew because of a discomfort with their daughters' sexuality. The daughters interpreted dad's absence as a sign of their own failure—that they were unable to please. The only explanation they have for the breakdown in the relationship with their dads is their puberty. For girls, physical maturation is traumatic enough, but when they also perceive that it means they cannot be close to their fathers, it becomes even less inviting. Some, who unconsciously long for their earlier years and the illusion of being daddy's little girl, may limit their eating to stop or reverse the growing up process.

Men usually have an easier time relating to daughters before they look sexual or become interested in boys. A father's unavailability or withdrawal may be especially powerful if the girl feels that her maturity destroys a bond between them. Patricia had many fond memories of her dad from early in her life. By the time she was eight or nine years old, however, he became distant. She wonders if her dad was afraid of her approaching puberty. His lack of emotional support during her formative adolescent years contributed to discomfort with her self, her sexuality, and relationships to men:

> I remember playing with him when I was little. He was fun and really liked small children. But I don't remember his presence in my middle years at all. He became sick and was very depressed, drinking, and retreating into himself. I never felt I had a real conversation with him. As an adolescent, I knew nothing about relating to males, although I was interested. I guess his absence was a big factor. It wasn't until graduate school that I learned how to relate to men. I believe my anorexia has a lot to do with this fear of sex.

Sometimes women who develop eating and body-image problems perceive that their parents, especially their fathers, do not approve of sex. These young women begin to feel that their bodies are evil and their impulses are immoral. They use self-destructive eating to bring themselves a less sexual body and diminish their guilt. As one woman said:

> I knew if I reached a certain weight I wouldn't have to worry about doing wrong—no one would be attracted to me so I wouldn't have any guilt. It was a way to work around the guilt . . . . I knew my father's attitudes about sex. I felt I should be punished for being curious about sex and interested in guys, that I was bad, nothing good in me. Not eating was a way to take things out on myself.

Many female teenagers today dread their physical changes because they assume that physical maturity means they should be ready and willing to have intimate relationships. Since they have desperately hoped to please their fathers, they cannot imagine being able to say "no" to men. Their solution is to abuse themselves through not eating, excess exercise, or other self-destructive behaviors so they will be unattractive. They have no way to cope other than to reject their bodies, their sexuality, and their need for food.

For some, an eating disorder reflects both an interest in and an anxiety about sexuality, a conflict that arises from experiences within their families, "I was very fearful of sex. All of my parents' taboos and limits seemed to really cover their fears of my sexuality. I was afraid but I wanted it. My anorexia was a way to delay having sex."

One woman, whose problems with food began after her first sexual relationship, described that her eating was a way of dealing with her guilt, her discomfort, and her inability to assert her needs:

> Sex was real scary to me. My anorexia has more to do with that than with food. Once I was involved sexually I thought I had to marry my boyfriend. But it wasn't a good relationship. It wasn't at all satisfying. I saw it as another performance. I really felt guilty and bad about the sex. That may have been why I stopped eating. I had never really known my father, although he was there. Maybe if I had felt close to him, my relationships with other men would have been better.

These words reveal how unsatisfied father hunger impairs feelings about sexuality and therefore affects relationships with other men. If this woman had had positive experiences relating to her father as a person, she might have been able to negotiate her first sexual encounter more successfully. Instead, she could not set limits and experienced tremendous guilt. She could, however, set limits on her eating, and this lessened the guilt. When she finally began to explore the disappointments she felt with her father, she discovered the underlying reasons for her problems with sex and food.

FATHER HUNGER AND EARLY MATURATION

Girls who enter puberty early may be a special risk to develop eating problems and body dissatisfaction. Early maturation is very disruptive to girls. They feel different from their peers and may worry whether they will be able to maintain friendships or if they will be ostracized for their unique bodies. These girls will be extremely self-conscious, fretting about how to cover up the signs of puberty—breasts and menstrual periods.

Early maturers will also be the target of teasing by boys, and sometimes by adult men. This makes them feel more ashamed of their figures. Often, the end result is a generalized feeling of being out of control in all aspects of their lives. Since their bodies are doing new and unpredictable things, they expect the same kind of uncertainty and powerlessness across the board. Neither the daughter nor her parents are ready for her to have a teen-aged body when she is nine or ten years old. Fathers may be particularly uneasy and unsure when this happens. They may withdraw more dramatically and quickly when their little girl becomes a woman as early as the fourth or fifth grade.

The eating and body-image difficulties associated with early maturation are visible in the story of Nicole, who developed an eating disorder when she was fourteen. She had matured when she was ten. She remembers that her puberty happened quickly. In fact, she described that she "went to bed one night after playing with dolls and woke up the next morning with breasts." She had always been shy and reserved, and felt more uncomfortable about the male attention she was getting as she developed physically. Her new breasts attracted much attention from the adult men in her life—her father, his friends, her uncles, and strangers as well. She recollects that once she developed, the expectations she perceived from others changed dramatically. She felt she was being forced to act like an adult woman, but still wanted to play with dolls:

I wasn't ready for my body. Nobody mentioned this as part of growing up, but once my body changed, everyone started responding to me differently, even adult men—friends of my father's. I just thought this is the way it is. This is how life is going to be. I hadn't changed—my body just looked different and people were only responding to that. I didn't feel I had any control over it. I decided I should just look a certain way—the way I thought they wanted—so I started to lose weight. I got even more attention then. Each time, I hadn't changed inside but people were responding to me differently. It seemed that people only cared about my body, not about me.

Nicole felt she had little control over her destiny once she had a sexual body. During her first dating experience, the boy, who was a few years older than she, was physically violent with her and tried to rape her. She recalls that this trauma marked the beginning of her eating problems, but believes that if she had experienced a more affirming relationship with her father, perhaps she would have felt a greater sense of control over her body and her life. Hungry for male approval, she felt no capacity to refuse when this man took advantage of her. She began to believe that becoming an adult woman "was not very enticing," and that it would bring her less, not more, control over her life.

By the time Nicole was a college student, when I first met her, she recognized that although she had made much progress in overcoming her eating disorder, she still had some difficulty handling relationships with men. She was afraid of getting close to men, so she dated only casually, not seriously. Even now, she is very critical of her body and afraid of sexual intimacy because she expects disapproval and rejection.

Since Nicole started therapy and began to acknowledge her feelings about her dad, she has made much progress in many areas, including the relationship with him, and anticipates that she will continue to get better. The positive changes she has experienced with her father since she has worked on this relationship give her confidence that other interactions with men will improve.

Nicole's story is representative of the serious consequences father hunger can have on a daughter's adolescent development. As I listened to Nicole describe her father, my image of him was not of a man who deliberately rejected his daughter or who has negative attitudes toward women and their bodies. He sounded like an average man who had no idea what his daughter needed from him. Again, we are reminded of the discrepancies between male and female experiences and values. If only her father's upbringing had not been so traditionally masculine, he might have understood how important he was to her, and she might have avoided the anguish of her eating disorder. Instead, it offered her the only way to cope with the disappointment she experienced with her body and with men.

FATHER HUNGER AND SEXUAL TRAUMA

As we have seen, eating and body-image problems are often the result of unhealthy attitudes and feelings about sexuality conveyed by the family or culture. In many cases, inappropriate sexual experiences lead to disordered eating and body dissatisfaction.

Exact data about the incidence of sexual trauma affecting women with food and body-image problems are impossible to attain because such violence is generally under-reported. Some victims are afraid of repercussions should they disclose it. Others are ashamed and fearful of having provoked or caused the abuse. Still others cope by denying the event. Often, people who have been victimized have defended themselves against the pain so completely that they can only remember it after months or years of therapy. Nevertheless, the powerful and confusing feelings evoked by sexual trauma certainly contribute to eating and body-image conflicts. Starving or binging and purging may be efforts to establish personal boundaries, to punish oneself (people who have been abused often make sense of it by convincing themselves that they deserved or provoked it), to express anger, or to control one's life.

Although the incidence figures vary and may not be completely accurate for the reasons mentioned above, reports of the association between disordered eating and sexual abuse are sufficient to warrant our concern. In one study of bulimia, 21% of the sample reported that a difficult sexual experience had precipitated their eating problems.[1] In another group of 172 adult bulimic female outpatients, 66% had been physically victimized; 46% had been physically or sexually abused as children, and one third of these were later victimized as adults.[2] Another study also reports the incidence of sexual abuse in 66% of females with eating disorders.[3] At least 40% of the adolescent and young adult women in the treatment program I direct have suffered a sexual trauma, either rape or molestation.

A man who violates the accepted physical boundaries with his daughter causes severe anguish. Children expect to be protected by parents, especially by their fathers, so an incestuous relationship with father does not feel right or safe. Shame and self-remorse dominate the victim's psyche and the daughter will blame herself for his transgressions. Also, her belief that she must obey her father compels her to participate as long as he wants her to do so. She will usually be bound to secrecy, with dad threatening something she perceives as more devastating should she refuse.

The relationships within the family become warped. Even if other family members suspect or know about the abuse, they deny it to maintain the family's delicate, albeit dysfunctional, balance. The mother-daughter relationship will be especially marred. Complex, often contradictory emotions—jealousy, gratitude, rage, insecurity, self-blame, fear, neediness, isolation, depression, love, dread—all interact to paralyze the family in its patterns. Often, disordered eating is the only way the daughter can feel a sense of control over her body and can discharge her pent-up anger and despair. Her need to take care of her family supersedes her right for sexual self-determination. She will act in a way that does not threaten family harmony. Abusing her body is her maladaptive, but loving response.

Sexual traumas awaken many feelings about the father-daughter relationship, even when the perpetrator is not the father but a family friend, relative, or boyfriend. The young woman feels let down by her dad, since, as our cultural myths promise, he was not there to protect her, nor had he taught her how to handle such advances by men. The daughter undergoes renewed feelings of abandonment, but is afraid to tell her father; she anticipates that he will blame and disappoint her once more. The more distant her father has been historically, the more overwhelming the effects of sexual abuse will be.

Sexual traumas generalize to a mistrust of all men. If the daughter's relationship with her father is already distant, it will only become more so after such an incident because she will withdraw from him. Puzzled by this, he may then be more unsure how to approach her, and therefore, unable to give her support and provide corrective experiences at a time when she needs them dearly. Again, the divergent psychologies of men and women are at work, and fathers, with their tendency to separate rather than to relate, unknowingly reinforce their daughters' distrust.

When fathers do provide support, the healing process following sexual trauma can be much easier. Furthermore, when men are involved in caring for young children (below the age of three), they are less likely to sexually abuse their own or other children.[4] An early intimate relationship, therefore, seems to keep men from becoming abusers, and may equip them with the sensitivity necessary should such events occur.

Since the father-daughter bond serves as a prototype for other attachments, it is important for women with eating problems and for victims of abuse to understand more about this relationship.

For example, if a daughter doesn't feel loved, she may act provocatively to try to assure herself attention from other men. Her attempt to satisfy her father hunger may increase the possibility of a later sexual trauma.

Therapists working with eating disordered patients need to be sensitive to the possibility of abuse, past or present, and need to help their patients come to terms with the physical violations they have experienced. Conversely, mental health professionals who treat women with histories of sexual abuse should inquire about the patients' eating habits and be certain that additional help be provided if an eating problem is present. In all cases, clinicians and patients should try to comprehend how the trauma reflects and affects the father-daughter relationship.

Father hunger complicates the normal psychosexual development of the young woman. She experiences the process of maturation as one of displeasure, for it juxtaposes a drive to relate to men with her awareness of her dad's distance. Hoping to understand her father and connect with him somehow, she will attribute his indifference, or his inappropriate interest, to her new sexual characteristics. Her body becomes the explanation for his behavior. Feelings of loss surrounding her relationship to him begin to distort logic, and the young woman begins to reason: "If only my body were different, I'd have a better relationship with dad." She believes that being smaller, thinner, less or more attractive, less or more muscular, will change their interactions and will please him. If not, maybe it will please some other man somewhere. Thus, discomfort in her relationship with her father evolves into discomfort with her physical self and into changes in her eating.

This system of logic has devastating effects. The impact of father hunger distorts her feelings about her body, which in turn leads her to reject her basic and natural appetites for sex and for food. Any impulses must be controlled, because her sexuality is unacceptable. Food, the fuel for her body, is forbidden. The fundamental pleasure of eating, something most of us take for granted, vanishes from their lives. This is especially true for women whose father hunger is intensified by sexual trauma, as you will see in the two case studies that follow.

CAROL: "My anger is really with my father."

Carol's story demonstrates how sexual abuse, eating, body image, and father hunger interact, potentially leading to anger turned inward, against the self, through bulimia. Although her father was not the perpetrator, she felt he was responsible because of the minimal role he played in her life. She went on to repeat the pattern of victimization in several relationships until she grasped the horror of her family's experience. For years, fasting and binging and purging were her only methods of dealing with her rage.

One of three children, Carol grew up in an intact family, but her father was chronically ill and depressed. Family life was very unpleasant. Prior to developing her eating disorder, she was molested by her older brother. She blamed this on the passivity and noninvolvement of her father:

> He was aloof, insensitive, unaware of our feelings and what was going on in our lives. My brother took over his role—he was a tyrant, mean, and demanded everything of me, even sex. No one protected me from him. As I got older, I kept on getting involved with men like my brother. It was the only way I knew how to be with men. I'm sure this would have been different if my father had done more with me . . . I know I really wanted approval from men and that was the only time my brother had shown affection. I picked a lot of men who hurt me and I was always trying to please them, not me. By being thin I was trying to be sexier for them.

Carol became very angry when she spoke about her brother's influence and power in the family. She described her father as a dejected, passive man and said that her older brother had become the authority figure in the house ("he even pushed my parents around"). Despite the fact that her brother was the "abuser," she stated:

> My anger is really with my father for not knowing me as a person and for not showing me he cared or that men can care in a noncoercive way. Until I could work this out and understand it, I ended up getting involved with men who abused me.

Like many other victims, Carol proceeded to repeat the trauma in other relationships. By adolescence, her pattern of otheration had been firmly established. The desires of men always superseded her own desires, even if the result was abuse of her body or her wishes.

Carol associated physical maturation with being abused. Because the maltreatment by her brother started when she was beginning to develop, she was "ashamed" of her sexual feelings. Fear of this appetite led her to also doubt her hunger for food. These two became linked together. She began extreme dieting. She would feel "high and virtuous" during fasting, which sometimes lasted as long as four days. This pattern alternated with periods of binging ("a way to eat myself to death and numb myself to the world") followed by vomiting ("to cleanse myself"). The poor self-image she had as a child was intensified by the relationship with her brother. She became extremely depressed and her eating disorder was a way to withdraw. For Carol, bleeding from her vomiting represented "a slow form of suicide."

Carol's symptoms intensified when she entered college and lived away from home. She got help from two counselors at college but it wasn't until she graduated and saw a therapist for long–term treatment that she began to make significant progress.

In her words, seeing a male therapist helped her "to form a better image of men." As I mentioned in describing Liz's therapy and recovery, having a male therapist sometimes helps break down the myths that men don't care about feelings or can't understand women and their problems.

Carol worked hard to understand the interactions among the abuse, her relationships with men, and her feelings about food and her body. During the course of her therapy, Carol's father died. Although she had been angry because her mother had ignored all the conflicts in the family, she gradually developed a better relationship with her. Carol believes that she had really recovered in many other ways, actually "in every other way," before the binging was over. Her bulimia had become a habit that she could only face and work on more directly after she began acknowledging her anger and developing insight about her family's problems and her responses to them. This took years of therapy and much work on her own as well. As she recovered, she was able to end the pattern of negative relationships with men in which they would either ignore her, as her father had, or abuse her, as her brother had. Her resentment and anger about the role her father played in the family had to become conscious before she could change her life.

Carol's story suggests that there are many paths to recovery. She had been sick for a long time but needed to understand family dynamics before she could get better. Others may need to control their symptoms before they can develop insight about the many factors contributing to their illness. I wonder if Carol's healing process would have been quicker or less painful if her family had entered treatment during her adolescence. Perhaps had their dynamics been identified earlier, Carol's bulimia could have been prevented, or at least could have been less deeply entrenched. For those of you who are suffering from anorexia, bulimia, or both, keep in mind that Carol's recovery took many, many years. She was sick for about 14 years and her recovery has been slow but quite complete.

Carol wishes her father had been alive so she could have talked to him as she worked through issues related to him during her recovery. Because of his death, she has lost that opportunity. With the help of a therapist, she found ways to process her feelings anyway. Letter-writing and other symbolic ways of speaking to her father facilitated this. Later, she confronted her brother about the abuse and her mother about her denial. Gradually, she has healed the wounds that led to her bulimia.

Carol's anger has subsided because she has taken the risky steps necessary to resolve it. She has had positive relationships with men wherein she asserted herself and expressed anger rather than turning it against herself. She has chosen a single lifestyle, but feels confident and comfortable negotiating differences and communicating feelings with both men and women.

JENNA: "I could control what I ate."

Jenna's story also includes incidences of sexual trauma and her words may help you to see how an eating disorder can be a means of coping with the feelings, particularly the loss of control, brought on by such victimization.

Eating became Jenna's language because it gave her a feeling that she was controlling her life after her father began to molest her. Food had been a very tightly managed commodity during Jenna's childhood. Money was limited and Jenna felt that her parents dominated her through what they allowed her to eat, while blaming this on sparse resources. Food intake was an easy way of expressing herself and trying to regain control. Although it was her father who molested her, Jenna was angry with both of her parents:

> My father molested us and my mother would sit there and watch. When I asked her for help she'd say, "He is your father, he is not hurting you." I couldn't control that at all. I could control what I ate. That's how my undereating started.

Jenna's mother was passive and seemed to agree with everything Jenna's father did. Her dad appeared overly interested in sexuality and this made her self-conscious about her own sexual development:

> My father was always talking about sex. He's the one who explained the facts of life to us. I remember thinking about all the people he would tell when I got my period and all the jokes he would make. Maybe if I had a better relationship with him, he would not have used sex—the jokes and the molestation—as ways to get close.

Because of her father's constant remarks about sexuality, Jenna had difficulty feeling comfortable about herself as her body matured. She felt guilty about her interest in sex and about all of her needs. Then, when she was 17, her unmarried sister became pregnant and her father became even more concerned about Jenna's sexuality. ("He was always accusing me of things I didn't do.")

Jenna developed a severe case of anorexia as a response to this sexual trauma and lack of support in her relationship with her father. By starving herself, she intended to control her anger and her body. She wanted to be more in charge of her life, no longer dominated by her father's demands, which now included sex. Food was the only thing she could control, but it served another purpose: it punished her for wanting a relationship other than what her father could give, and for being unable to achieve this on her own.

Throughout her early adulthood, her father hunger and self-rejection persisted and Jenna developed many negative relationships with men. She would do anything for them, including trying to change her body or lose weight to please them. Like many women with eating disorders, she was both interested in and terrified of sex. Her father's emphasis on her sexuality and his accusations made this a highly charged issue for her. She saw herself as being at the mercy of her own curiosity and of her father's impulses, rather than as in charge of her own destiny.

Years later, Jenna has recovered in many ways. Physically, she has returned to the weight she was before she stopped eating. She developed a positive relationship with a man, married him, and now has a family. She also has a professional job which she enjoys. She worries about her children's relationship with her husband and tries to foster an active role for him and to share responsibility with him. Jenna is a conscientious and thoughtful woman, spouse, and parent who has struggled to find a comfortable way to control her life without being too rigid.

Her father's criticisms, distance, and inappropriate sexual behaviors remain open wounds, and Jenna's efforts to better understand her relationship with him have occurred without his taking part. Although he never participated in therapy, most of the fathers I have seen will, if their daughters or their daughters' therapists communicate to them how important they are in the process. Her father was certainly instrumental in her life, but she has had to heal and take charge of her life without the benefit of his involvement in understanding and rebuilding their relationship.

CHAPTER 8

◆ ◆ ◆

THE FAMILY'S
FUNCTIONAL DYSFUNCTION

The father hunger that pervades contemporary western society results in unfulfilling, frustrating roles for all family members. They have had to develop ways to interact and maintain themselves without men actively involved at home. In essence, fatherless families find dysfunctional ways to be together in order to function at all. I call this functional dysfunction: operating in a manner that works successfully at a superficial level but is not satisfying, productive, or conducive to personal growth and interpersonal relationships on a deeper level.

Loyalty to the myths about mothers' and fathers' roles may result in a lifestyle that looks good and is successful in the world. Yet, the scene is not as pretty on the inside. Parents usually do not feel supported by each other, mothers feel burdened, fathers feel excluded, and children do not receive the love, security, and acceptance they deserve. Daughters may cope with this inner emptiness by eating to fill themselves up or by starving, because they believe they do not deserve to be full. Their eating reflects their emotions.

Families mirror the prevailing social beliefs and norms. If they are functionally dysfunctional, then our culture is as well. The families in this book replicate the skewed distribution of power in our society: men have it in the world, so women usually have to find it elsewhere—within the family or via their bodies. When an adolescent worries about her future as an adult female, the achievement of a "perfect" body, disciplined exercise, or weight loss may emerge as goals.

Almost every woman who suffers from eating problems, body-image dissatisfaction, and weight preoccupation, experiences these patterns of functional dysfunction. The paradox for these individuals and families is similar to the double-bind that fathers in our culture experience: the more empty and unsatisfying their internal life is, the more successful they appear to be in the world. In fact, women with eating disorders systematically report that when they look their best to others, they are actually doing their worst in terms of symptoms, depression, despair, loneliness, and hopelessness. In this chapter, we examine why this functional dysfunction occurs and how some individuals will wage war with their bodies and their appetites as a result.

COMMON PATTERNS IN FAMILIES WITH EATING PROBLEMS

When we study families whose members have developed severe eating problems, body-image dissatisfaction, and weight preoccupation, we do not find one singular family type. In fact, the family is only one of many forces that collide in an individual's life to lead to such suffering. Furthermore, we don't study them until the problem has become deeply entrenched, so we don't always know whether the family interaction preceded the problem or resulted from it. Eating problems are extremely challenging for families, and parents may respond with ineffective coping mechanisms because they are so worried or overwhelmed. The stress of the eating disorder may lead to new dysfunctional interactions.

Thus, how a family functions is both a contribution and a consequence.

Some common patterns in families with eating and body-image problems do exist, however, and because each person and family is a unique blend of the many influences affecting them, these dynamics will express themselves in different ways and to varying degrees in each case. Since other authors have reviewed these patterns in detail,[1-5] they need only to be summarized here.

First, families with functional dysfunction avoid conflict as much as they can. Mothers strive to keep the family running smoothly, since their role is the day-to-day maintenance of relationships. They want their husbands to see what a good job they're doing, but may define that in terms of children who achieve, have few needs, please adults, and never fight. Fathers, invested in how well they provide for the family, will expect gratitude and serenity at home, so children learn to tip-toe around dad. Mothers frequently say things like, "Don't upset your father," unknowingly contributing to the distance between fathers and children. Usually, conflicts between the parents or between parents and children either are not identified or are ignored. Communication is stunted or minimal, and the family tends to deny and avoid problems just to "keep the peace."

In these families, parental authority is seen as absolute and unquestionable. No disagreements or hot issues can be discussed, so children do not learn how to negotiate a position for themselves. Girls will feel especially powerless as they see their parents act out these roles, because they are particularly aware of the family's emotional tone. Their brothers, conditioned to be more independent, may not be as concerned with family dynamics and usually find ways to assert themselves outside the home. Girls will face two major dilemmas when they recognize that their families have problems. First, they blame themselves, and second, they experience impotence and ineffectiveness because they can't make things better.

We see some differences in why conflicts appear and how they are manifested in anorexic and bulimic families. Those afflicted by anorexia reflect many of the patterns described above—they are so adept at denying problems that they truly do not see or feel the tensions within the family. People get along with each other, at least superficially. In families with bulimic daughters, conflicts may be more visible and the home-life is often chaotic, disorganized, and stressful. Despite this awareness, however, no resolution occurs and the relationships suffer.

In both family constellations, because of the peripheral position the father holds, parents do not share responsibilities. The frustration resulting from this lack of problem-solving becomes the backdrop for the family's emotional life. People do not feel good about themselves when they avoid obstacles instead of mastering them. In these homes, trust and emotional support take the "back seat" to presenting a positive impression to the outside world. Being honest about one's own feelings is considered a betrayal of the family. Loyalty to the establishment supersedes self-disclosure. Communication is stifled.

Within the anorexic or bulimic system, family members become entangled with each other because individual identity is poorly defined. Boundaries between immediate members and between generations are weak. Children may end up taking care of the adults, since they do not know how to articulate their own feelings or desires. Although they may want more contact with mom or dad, they will be unable to express this directly. Family members have little "space" or privacy, and again, an individual's needs are sacrificed for the group. Resulting from this pattern of conflict avoidance and constricted communication is pseudomutuality, where family members pretend that "everything is OK," but at great cost to themselves.

When families exhibit inadequate intergenerational boundaries, parents have difficulty distinguishing children's needs from their own. One or both may become overly close to the child. This pattern is potentially disastrous, because it keeps parents from facing any problems within their marriage. Marital dissatisfaction is common in eating disordered families, but the parents do not deal with this directly. Instead, because of the blurred boundaries, the child becomes a best friend to one of the parents or tries to bring them together through her symptoms. Losing weight, becoming unhealthy, and binging or purging may be unconscious attempts to get parents' attention and keep them focused on a shared predicament.

When a child is pulled into a marriage in this way, we call it triangulation. Instead of parents dealing with any problems between them as a couple, a third party gets in the middle of their communications. The system does not allow for privacy or separateness. Dyads do not exist—all relationships will be triangles. Even when an issue occurs between one parent and a child, the other parent will become involved. These interactions are unhealthy because people are not dealing directly with the problem or with each other. Conflicts rarely become resolved. Also, the more a child is triangulated into marital issues, the less she will be involved in normal activities that are more satisfying and developmentally appropriate.

Triangulation severely handicaps children, and females will express this through misuse of food and their bodies. The more a daughter caretakes her family, the less apt she is to progress normally and to move away from her parents during adolescence. An eating disorder or conflicts about body maturation and appearance may be the only safe way for her to express that something is wrong with the family's functioning. In fact, most eating problems develop during adolescence, when children traditionally leave the family nest. They cannot easily proceed with their own lives until some of these problems are addressed.

If families can view an eating or body-image conflict as a sign of functional dysfunction and as an attempt to cope with cultural myths and multigenerational traditions that just don't fit their needs, they usually can help the person suffering, as well as themselves. In fact, they can use the problem to find ways to improve their relationships rather than to blame themselves or each other. As we discussed early in this book, families are complicated systems wherein no one person causes the problem. Thinking about single causes is not very helpful when we are dealing with such a complex reality as a woman's relationship to food or to her body. Instead, it is helpful if families look at how their acceptance of the culture, beliefs, and traditions surrounding them has compromised their happiness. What we often find is that our shared father hunger and desire for more personally satisfying roles for men and women underlie the family's veneer and functional dysfunction.

PARENTAL ROLES

It is not just the children who suffer from father hunger; both parents are carrying the same sense of disappointment surrounding their fathers. Furthermore, since father hunger is a cultural tradition handed down from one generation to the next, this loss is not a conscious one. Men and women enter parenting with a handicap that even they may not recognize. This limitation will affect all of their interactions with their spouses and children. How can a man who was not fathered know how to parent? How can a mother who also was not fathered help her husband have a constructive, involved, emotionally-attached connection to their children?

Unfortunately, few couples have been able to overcome the impact of father hunger in their parenting. Instead, most families adjust and live a life of functional dysfunction. Mothers tend to do too much to compensate for their husbands' absence. As wives, they feel overburdened and overextended and need help from their husbands, but their background of father deprivation keeps them from asking; they feel they have no right to request more from men. Men continue to feel isolated and unimportant to the family. As fathers, they underfunction and feel left out, isolated, and unimportant. Each parent may want more from the other but doesn't know how to ask for this. This leads to bitterness and hostility between them. Again, no one finds satisfaction.

This is the template young women are given for their lives. They grow up knowing that they will carry most of the day-to-day responsibilities for their families. Furthermore, they believe that they have no control over the situation, and feel angry about this heritage. They are resentful because their mothers need them to help with the house and other family responsibilities. They also feel guilty because they sense their mothers' burdens. Wanting more from dad and being angry with mom easily translates itself into food conflicts. Jessica describes how these mixed emotions led to her severe eating problems and rejection of her body:

> I felt guilty all the time—guilty because I was angry with mom for needing me to help—guilty for wanting more time with my dad. I hated myself—I thought I was bad for having these feelings. I would punish myself by not eating. Then I'd crave food and overeat. I thought I was the problem and that there was something wrong with me. Now I know it was because my dad was just never there. My mother and I both needed more from him than he could give. But he was a "good father" by our society's standards.

Jessica's family was a perfect example of functional dysfunction and the negative consequences of father hunger. On the outside, they were a perfect, successful family, a "pillar in the community." They "had everything." Her father ran the business handed down from his family and made lots of money. Her mother was a "model" homemaker whose home, social, and community responsibilities left little time or energy for herself. Her parents operated in different spheres, coming together only for social purposes and for the children; they did not share responsibilities. Her mother was overwhelmed but accepted this knowing that her lifestyle was the family tradition and the cultural dictate. Unable to ask her husband for help, Jessica's mother demanded a great deal from her. In turn, Jessica spent her adolescence resenting her mother and dreading adulthood. As an adult, Jessica has come to realize how her father contributed to her feelings, but for years she lived in anger with her mother and in conflict about being a woman. The following quote reveals her confused perceptions:

> My father was in his own world—work and golf. My mother had too much to deal with—all of the kids and the responsibilities for the family.... One of the most damaging things was that we were so sheltered and protected—our parents never let us know the pressures that were going on. My mother also made my father look like a god. It was so unfair. It was the opposite of what was really happening.

Once she understood the role her father had in the family's life and how his culturally-endorsed script kept him from understanding and supporting her mother, Jessica was able to make peace with her mother and herself. Gradually, she was able to eat with less conflict and to accept her body and her femininity.

Jessica's experience is common to women who suffer from eating and body-image conflicts. A girl who grows up seeing her mother receive little thanks or recognition can easily develop negative feelings about the prospects of being an adult woman. Women's greatest assets—caring for others, nurturing, and relating—are not even rewarded at home, so what are the prospects of their being recognized in a world that is based on masculine principles and power? The burdens of femininity do not look attractive and the payoffs are few. This may lead to a rejection of the physical changes accompanying maturation or a desire to return to childhood.

Frequently, therapists hear women state that they do not want a life like their mother's. They do not want to sacrifice so much to please others and to take care of their families with little help. They may decide to avoid men or may be unable to find a balance in heterosexual relationships. Many act out their ambivalence about being a woman through their bodies and food. As one woman told me:

> I didn't want a life like my mother's so I didn't want a body like hers. I didn't want the same kind of relationships and I didn't think I could find any other way. So I rejected my body and retreated from the world. Maybe if my parents had had a different kind of relationship I would have felt okay about becoming a woman. I blame my dad a lot. If he had been a different kind of husband, I probably would have had a different life. Maybe I wouldn't have had all these problems with food and my body.

A CHILD'S SOLUTION

Children sometimes develop problems in order to get their parents to solve their differences and work together as a unit. Family therapists treating many different kinds of problems see this phenomenon repeatedly. When children develop eating problems or compromise their health in another way, parents usually rally together to address the issue. Yet, much of the unhappiness is rooted in the unsatisfying roles the parents play and the long-term consequences of father's absence in the family.

Linda is a good example of this. She blamed herself for her parents' strained relationship and for their inability to communicate with each other. Linda's mother had had a breakdown during Linda's childhood and her father tried to make family life as conflict-free as possible. Her mother tended to be very emotional and to "fly off the handle" but her stoic father rarely shared his feelings. She often felt confused by her parents' interactions. Although her mother said her dad was in charge, in reality her mother ran the show. She felt responsible for this problem and used her eating to punish herself.

> Mother always put father in a leadership role, but they were really playing a game. I always knew my father was just doing what she wanted. I felt I was a problem between them. I felt guilty, in the middle of them, and thought I should punish myself. I stopped eating.

Linda was anxious for her parents to work out the conflicts she perceived. She had grown up feeling insecure and unprotected because of her parents' fights and inability to share parenting. They, however, were unable to admit their problems and acted as if everything was fine. This confused Linda. She blamed herself for their problems but also condemned herself for her perceptions. She had begun to feel that there was no place for her, either in her family or out in the world. Through treatment she was able to stop the cycle of self-blame and to accept the roles they chose to maintain.

Linda now believes that her eating disorder is directly related to her parents' patterns of interaction and emotional expression. Her troubles did not arise only from having a perfectionist, strict, demanding mother or from having a non-expressive, stern father, but also from the ways in which her parents interacted. Her eating was a way to get her father more involved in the family and to clarify who was in charge.

> I felt if dad had been more involved before, it might not have been as severe, may not have happened. . . . I saw my father come into my life when I got sick. Although it was presented that he was head of the household, it just wasn't so. I wanted him to be more involved because I felt he understood more than mom did.

In this way, an eating disorder can be a plea for the father to be more present and available. It is also a request for change in the family. Until the underlying issues were addressed in some way, bingeing, starving, over exercising, and purging were the only ways Linda could safely express pain.

PARENTS, POWER, AND FOOD

Food is a potentially strong medium for self-expression in all families, but for some it will become their primary means of exerting power and control. Many women use food as a weapon, their only defense in a world they experience as unfriendly. How does eating gain such power and how does it reflect the functional dysfunction we see in these families?

Many factors coalesce to give food a strong influence in families and between parents. In infancy, food is the first and most frequent demand of the child. The ways in which parents respond to the infant's hunger will affect her expectations of subsequent relationships. She will develop a preset notion as to whether interactions with caregivers will be satisfying or frustrating, consistent or chaotic. As the child grows older, parents may become more aware of how they can use food to control behavior. Similarly, the child will see eating as an area in which to challenge parental authority.

Often these interactions reflect how the parents' families used food with them. For example, if they were raised in an environment with a great deal of parental control over eating, they will probably repeat the pattern. Also, if they are dieting or struggling with their weight or body image, they may unknowingly convey negative attitudes about food, may even underfeed young children, or be critical of the child's natural appetite. If the parents have opposing attitudes or behaviors surrounding food, this can be confusing to the children, who may not know when and how to eat or even whether their appetites should be satisfied.

Fathers of infants often feel very left out of the closeness and warmth of the feeding process, especially if the mother is breast-feeding. As the child gets older, the dad may try to become involved around food in order to develop an emotional connection. Unfortunately, they usually wait until there is a problem!

When they child is not eating well, dad may step in and try to force-feed the youngster. This is a frequent pattern in families with eating disordered children and adolescents. Such controlling and punitive efforts rarely work, for by that time, eating has assumed tremendous importance in the young person's psyche. Food refusal has generated a welcome response from dad, and the behavior may continue in order to maintain his attention.

Young people who compulsively overeat may also want their dads to intervene, but overeating rarely elicits the response they seek. Parents may be critical and even act disgusted when children eat too much, but seldom do they examine how their family's emotional functioning, their structure around food, and their attitudes toward their children's bodies encourage these behaviors. In any case, whether children are undereating, chaotically eating, or overeating, they are expressing important needs that are not understood or met. Often these include feelings of depression and low self-esteem due to the father's unavailability.

In many families, mealtime is the singular occasion when they come together and children see their fathers. Unfortunately, this is also a time when punishments and criticisms are dispensed and conflicts are expressed. Food becomes less enjoyable and more conflictual the more it is associated with the bad news of the day. When I ask adults with eating problems about their family's meals, I usually hear how unpleasant these were. As one woman told me:

> Mealtime was the only opportunity to fight in front of dad. I think we all hoped he would jump in and solve our problems. Instead, he yelled at us about grades and homework, about how tired he is at the end of the day, and how horrible it was to come home to us. He would scream about our not appreciating all he did for us.

Unconscious, powerful associations emerge in these situations. Soon, food and eating represent tension and conflict.

Instead of feeling satisfaction when they come together for meals, they feel disapproval, disconnection, and discomfort. If this is the only time children spend with their dads, we can see how an appetite for food, and hunger for daddy, can become intertwined.

Meals also may evoke conflicts because they are the times when men and women come together in their traditional roles as providers and nurturers. Mothers continue to do most of the cooking today, and many feel overburdened and resentful. At the same time, they have great difficulty allowing their husbands to help them in this area. After all, the kitchen has represented power and identity to women for centuries and it's hard to give that up. As one feminist said, "While you can take the woman out of the kitchen, can you really take the kitchen out of the woman?"[6]

Girls who grow up in an ambiance where women are in charge of meals and men have a smaller contribution, learn to assert themselves through food. Resentful of the role handed down to them to cook and care for others, they may express this by ignoring their own hunger and needs. Thus, food preparation is another dimension reflecting the damaging consequences of the division of labor and the absence of father from the day-to-day operations of the family.

The following story of Laura, a young woman who has recovered from self-starvation, illustrates many of these tensions. Her family was successful and admired by others. On the outside, they looked very happy and functional; but on the inside, they were miserable, emotionally disconnected, and dysfunctional. Her parents never shared responsibilities. Her mother was tired and angry and her father was oblivious to this and to the damaging results of his peripheral role in their home. Laura could only express her pain through food. Her physical emptiness reflected an emotional abyss. Her parents, thankfully, heard her pain and worked hard to open up the communication in the family. Their lifestyle exemplifies the impact of father hunger and the need to understand family problems and conflicts with food and body image from a larger, systems perspective.

LAURA: "My anorexia was a challenge to my father, to get him more involved."

In order to understand why she developed such a serious eating disorder, Laura had to explore the transgenerational patterns in her family—the values, interactional styles, roles, problems, and coping mechanisms handed down from one generation to the next. Fortunately, Laura's parents willingly participated in therapy with her. This helped her to understand the family mold, gave her permission to free herself from what didn't work for her, and enabled her to create new ways of "being" that would end the emptiness of starvation, and lead to a fuller life.

As she looks back on her childhood, Laura remembers nothing unusual about how her family treated food *per se*. She had always been a good eater and was willing to try any food. Mealtime, however, was the only time she saw her father and the only time the family came together.

> Food wasn't a big issue, but dinner was the focus of family life. The dinner table was the emotional cauldron where all hell broke loose. I was usually the center of that. I think my anorexia was a challenge to my father, to get him more involved. I had always expressed my conflict with my mother at the dinner table, for the same reason.

She describes her parents as being very controlling. Any expression of feelings was denied. The family atmosphere had been like this for generations, and Laura explains that "control simply became a part of me" which logically extended to her eating and her anorexia.

Her father, especially, conveyed that "feelings are not allowed." When he was present, usually only at dinner time, he was setting limits, "You couldn't win. He'd say, calm down; speak up. I just couldn't win. He had tremendous authority and power over the family."

Laura felt ignored, unimportant, and confused. She wanted to live up to their expectations but her parents never broke through their poor communication pattern to tell her that they were satisfied with her efforts or that they thought she was "good enough."

Part of Laura's family heritage was a concern about physical appearances. As Laura became an adolescent, she not only experienced the pressure from peers and from our culture to focus on appearance and to be thin, but she also received this message repeatedly from her family, who considered thinness a positive sign of self-control and achievement. Laura did not feel good about herself, nor did she feel her parents' acceptance and love. So these cultural communiques about the value of being thin assumed even greater power in her life.

In addition to the pressure to be thin and the focus on emotional control and appearances in her family, Laura was to experience another very significant problem. Her twin sister had some genetically-based physical handicaps that affected her growth and sexual development which made Laura more aware of her own body. Her sister received experimental medical treatments during her adolescence and Laura was often evaluated at the same time to provide a basis of comparison. She was never asked how she felt about this, as the family's emotional energy went to her twin to help her through the medical procedures and adjust to her handicaps.

Laura's family experienced many stressors that were never discussed but that nevertheless overshadowed her needs. Moreover, the timing of her sister's more intense medical intervention coincided with their early adolescence and physical maturation. Also, at this time, the family moved to a new community and her mother returned to work. Laura began to feel she was being ignored and controlled even more than she had been in the past. Not only was she alone more of the time, but she was given increased responsibilities, which included cooking dinner. Family life was emotionally empty. Something had to change these patterns, and that something was anorexia:

> My anorexia shocked them into knowing I had feelings. They began to talk to me more. I needed affirmation and didn't have it inside of me. It first came from others and then from my parents.

Laura's eating disorder developed during her freshman year in college. In many areas in her life Laura was not allowed to make her own decisions. She attended a prestigious and very competitive women's college far from home, which was chosen by her parents. When she went away to school and was on her own for the first time, she was unsure of herself, and lonely.

For Laura, as for many others, the stresses preceding her eating problems had existed for many years, but the transition from home to college life stimulated the onset of symptoms. To make matters worse, she felt she had to handle her feelings and doubts alone because she could not express them to her family and had no other close relationships.

Laura had many new pressures to face, but her family was still focused on her sister. Although there are few undisputable facts in family therapy and adolescent development, the difficulties an adolescent has in separating from the family when there are obvious conflicts at home is a well-accepted psychological fact. Leaving for college was bound to be troublesome. She worried about her twin and felt guilty for being the "normal one." She was angry that her normalcy and competence had cost her any opportunity she might have had to receive her family's support.

Today, most schools recognize that students have problems. Many colleges now have extensive orientation and counselling programs to help students during the transition. Several have developed programs specifically for eating disorders, but Laura was attending college at a time when few services were available on campus.

Although she achieved academically, Laura still experienced pressure in a competitive college environment. She did not know what to do about her unhappiness and confusion. She felt abandoned, sad, and empty emotionally. By not eating, she stayed physically empty, which distracted her from an emotional void. In her words: "Food was an instrument of what I was experiencing—things I couldn't face directly."

She isolated herself from everyone, withdrawing into her dormitory room, locking the door, and studying constantly. She started cutting out certain foods. She remembers wanting to be more attractive but also struggling with thoughts of death and with questions about the value of her life. Paradoxically, her eating disorder reflected an openness and a desire for change and growth as well as a deep despair. She sees her anorexia as an internal battle between life and death.

> I had these life and death forces inside me—both sides were very active—they took me over. Till then my life was determined by my parents. Finally I had a life of my own and I was experiencing life and death warring inside me through the anorexia . . . . I didn't feel depressed but I had lots of thoughts about suicide—how I would do it, not that I would do it.

When she left for college, Laura was 5' 5" tall and weighed 115 pounds; in the spring she came home weighing 75 pounds. Her parents were shocked and gradually began to talk to her and support her as she struggled with decisions about transferring to another college. She was showered with attention and concern that previously had been reserved for her sister. Unfortunately, it took this crisis for her parents to be able to reach out to her in a way that felt loving and affirming. They entered family therapy:

My family could finally say things to each other. Communication opened up. Therapy should involve the whole family, not focus on the anorexic. Even if done in a supportive way, it feels like the anorexic is the rotten spot. I was feeling part of the family—we were working together. Before, I was only the emotional instigator. Things started to go better.

As Laura looks back, she realizes that a major stress in her family's life and in her development had been the inability of her parents to work together and support each other. They had never shared the responsibilities of raising the children, so the weight of Laura's sister's problems fell on her mother exclusively. Her father was doing what he was supposed to do—providing economically and staying out of the day-to-day family problems. It may have never occurred to him that he could help his wife in any way. But his wife, like many women, had the burden of the family as well as a new job outside the home. She was truly overwhelmed. The family legacy had not included any way for the parents to discuss these feelings and problems.

By default, Laura became the sounding board for her mother's anger and irritation. In addition, her mother expected Laura to take over any responsibilities she herself could not meet. Anger, resentment, and conflict filled the space between Laura and her mother; otherwise their relationship was devoid of emotional connection.

Because her father and mother could not work together, or as Laura put it, "the way the masculine and feminine clashed in the family," she was given a very difficult role, one that would compromise and confuse her development. Now Laura sees her eating disorder as a response to these family issues, especially the balance between the masculine and feminine.

I experienced the domination of both my parents in different ways.... I wasn't prepared for being on my own in college. Because they had been so domineering, I didn't know myself. But it was really because they couldn't come together and work together. My mother was in charge of the family but my father was in charge in a different way. They both tried to be in charge but they had a deep inability to understand each other. The masculine and the feminine clashed . . . . When I became anorexic I was trying to be more attractive and more sexual. I was struggling to be more feminine, but I had always been a tomboy. I was in conflict between my mother's life experience and my father's.

Since then Laura has had individual treatment in addition to the earlier family therapy. She has come to understand how the differences between her parents' life experiences contributed to the void she felt in her family and in herself. Understanding all of this helps her stop blaming herself and start to forgive them. The space between them has been filled by love and caring, so she no longer keep her body empty as an illustration of their functional dysfunction.

CHAPTER 9

◆ ◆ ◆

THE LEGACY OF LOYALTY

Loyalty to the accepted myths and traditions about men's and women's roles in families has great costs. As we have seen in earlier chapters, it allows father hunger to flourish and brings misery to all involved. Since we have all grown up indoctrinated by these myths, we know little about alternatives. Nor have we spent much time figuring out its lasting effects. They are, however, pervasive, insidious, and intangible. They compromise our connections, not only with dad but with other family members who also want more from him, and with relationships outside the home as well.

Children who grow up without dad's approval are plagued by self-doubt—that not good-enough feeling. This affects peer relationships, school achievement, behavior with adults, and many other aspects of interpersonal life. Furthermore, children come to disown parts of themselves. Instead of actualizing full potential, boys will reject their feminine side and girls will shun their masculine side. Lastly, all victims of father hunger suffer from feelings of guilt, grief, anger, loss, or alienation, but may be completely oblivious to the origins of these feelings. This is the legacy of loyalty, the undiscerning, sentimental allegiance to past beliefs about men and families.

COMPROMISED CONNECTIONS

An essential ingredient to healthy adolescence is the development of connections in new relationships. The young woman is not only relating to a new body, but psychosexual maturity also brings changes in interactions with parents, authority figures, other adults, peers, the social environment, and culture.

Parents who remain faithful to the traditional demands and myths about parenting are compromising all of these connections. Even though this adherence to the old ways is usually unconscious, it causes families to get stuck in old patterns of relating. They ignore each other's real needs and feelings without looking for effective solutions. For example, wives who want their children to have more of a relationship with their husbands may express this by nagging. They do not think they have permission to ask for more from men, so they cannot speak directly or assertively.

Taking this one step further, those women who do succeed in helping their children connect with their husbands may feel jealous, angry, or once more deprived of a special relationship with a man. So children, especially daughters, will suspect that a more satisfying relationship with father may carry a high price because mom will be angry. Being close to dad will mean losing mom. As a result, many daughters remain stuck and unfulfilled in their relationships to their fathers.

A daughter in these situations will work hard to please both parents. Often her most powerful desire is to bring mother and father together. She convinces herself that if she is the perfect daughter or has a perfect body, her parents will not only be happy with her but also with each other. In this way, her parents unhappiness has become her unhappiness as well as her focus in life. She is now effectively cut off from her own needs and feelings because of her family's ineffective patterns of interacting.

Her connections outside the family will also suffer as a result of this dysfunction at home. If she devotes her energy to solving family problems, pleasing her parents, and maintaining family roles, she won't have time to develop herself or her friendships. She will end up feeling empty, disconnected, and depleted. Although she may have superficial relationships with peers, a young woman growing up in this type of family will have compromised connections in all areas of relatedness.

DIVISION OF LABOR: DIVISION OF SELF

Loyalty to the old myths about parents' roles in families also contributes to a marked division of labor based on sex. Men and women grow up and survive in these systems by internally separating their masculine and feminine impulses from each other. These two dimensions do not come together in the family so they cannot come together in the self. Men reject their feminine side—all the nurturing, caring, emotive, and intimate behaviors associated with being female. Women shun their masculine side—the striving, performing, independent, and controlling attributes.

In order to adapt to this dysfunction, people disown important parts of themselves and discard their potential. For example, the family is "woman's work," so fathers don't try to be emotionally available to their children, and mothers often feel burdened by family life because making money or doing things away from home is primarily men's work. This division of labor can lead to dangerous divisions in relationships both to others and to the self.

This fragmentation affects a girl's interpersonal world, her self-concept and self-acceptance, but it also impacts how she feels about becoming part of the culture that promotes it. Afraid to venture out of the familiar, she will be increasingly affected by the dysfunction and divisiveness at home.

Young women with eating problems often describe the impact of the split between the masculine and feminine and the divided parenting that results: mothers nurture too much and fathers nurture too little, if at all. Frequently I hear comments like: "I know my mom got too close to me. I know it hurt me in the long run but she was only trying to make up for my dad. He was never there for either of us."

In these cases, the mothers become overly close or enmeshed with their daughters to make up for the lack of fathering. This compromises the daughter's development; she can't get to know herself because her mom is excessively involved in her life. It limits all of her relationships. The daughter feels guilty when she wants to develop close connections to other people; she knows how much mom loves her and she fears losing her. Instead, she abandons herself. She disowns her feelings, one of which is a desire to have a personal connection with her dad. Without a relationship with him, she has lost the possibility of knowing how to relate to men. The following quote illustrates how this can lead to an eating disorder:

> I know now that it wasn't right, but back then it seemed that my mother and I didn't need my father. We were perfect without him. But then, when I got to be a teenager, I had no way of dealing with men. I was petrified of losing my mother and petrified of growing up. But I knew I had to. I felt a battle between these sides of myself. I couldn't face these problems head on so I developed an eating disorder. Eventually, we all got help and the different parts of me could come together.

Another way families exhibit this division of labor occurs when a father tries to make contact with his daughter by buying her things. Being the economic provider isn't a sufficient basis for a fulfilling relationship, but the daughter feels guilty for wanting more. She will then try to deny these emotional needs. One woman described how this contributed to her eating problems:

On the outside, my dad was perfect. He bought me everything and I went to the right schools—other kids were always jealous. And I felt guilty about wanting more from him. I wanted a relationship, not just the trimmings. But I couldn't say that so I got sick instead. That got us into therapy and gradually we could talk. Now we've got a good relationship. But for years, I just felt bad about wanting more.

When families are excessively loyal to external standards, they deny their own needs and divide their emotional experience into what is and what is not acceptable. Girls will reject their desire for a relationship with dad because they've internalized the belief that he is unimportant. In order to control the hunger they have for him, they may try to deny their appetite for food as well.

GUILT

Part of the legacy of loyalty to the old ways is guilt. Everyone feels it. Mothers experience it because they bear the responsibility for the family's emotional life. Daughters encounter it because they believe they should be satisfied with what they are given and never ask for more. Fathers have it because they sense that they are useless in the family. When things go wrong they second-guess themselves, considering all the things they could or should have done.

Although men wrestle with guilt when their children are having problems, they have little responsibility for the day-to-day life of the family. Thus, they will feel less accountable and have more ways to escape the problems at home. Women will have more difficulty managing this emotion. A mother's culpability is based on what she has done; father's is based on his absence and, therefore, on what he has not done. Mothers, held liable for the family's well-being, question, "What did I do?" Fathers, removed from the inner workings of the family, think "If only I had been there, I could have changed everything." Absence-guilt and presence-guilt are very different experiences. It is helpful to understand these disparities as we address the myths about parenting and try to come up with new ways for mothers and fathers to work together.

To start, let's acknowledge that mothers consistently receive bad press in contemporary "pop psychology." When mothers seek help from therapists, guilt is the predominant theme. Unfortunately, they will hand down self-blame and remorse to their daughters, just as they bequeath cooking and homemaking to them. Why is guilt such a universal experience, especially for females? Again, the answer is found in the family's division of labor, where guilt and gender interact. Even the feminist literature and the family systems approach over-accentuate the importance of the mother-child dyad. This dyad is unrealistically presented as a separate entity from the family and from our cultural system. In fact, a recent analysis of articles in nine major clinical journals, including those devoted to family therapy and those written by women, found that mothers were blamed for 72 forms of psychopathology![1] This mother-bashing runs strong in our society even though there have been many changes in the traditional family structure, not the least of which is the fact that most families do not have a full-time mother at home. Women, however, easily accept the blame for their children's problems because they consider relationships their primary function and the emotional well-being of others their responsibility.

An example of the extent to which mother-bashing persists is the general understanding of incestuous families, where father is the perpetrator. Very often we blame the mother for not protecting the child from him. In fact, we often state that the mother contributed to the molestation because she was inadequate, distant, and was not satisfying her husband's sexual needs. We minimize the father's role by holding the mother accountable for his behavior, blaming her for the abuse her children have endured.

As a result, mothers often condemn themselves for their children's unhappiness and losses, even when they had no control over the events.

A father's guilt, based on his absence and the lost opportunities to protect his children or to provide emotionally, is a different phenomenon. Mothers experience regret, but fathers often feel empty, lacking, and confused about what they can contribute to their children. They react by maintaining the distance, a response that continues the pattern set by the legacy of loyalty.

As a result of these myths and attitudes, we find that both mothers and fathers are feeling blamed, misunderstood, inadequate, and wrong. This does not lead to strong, confident parenting, nor does it help parents to work out their problems together. Instead, our myths about mothers and fathers cause deep misunderstanding to develop between men and women. In turn, this contributes to young women's confusion about their future role as adults and uncertainty about their effectiveness and adequacy in their important relationships. Such feelings lay the groundwork for eating disorders.

Other sources of guilt will fertilize the seeds of eating and body-image problems as young women look forward to adulthood. Whether they choose to focus on career or on family life, or to combine the two, they can expect to feel inadequate. To understand how this happens, consider how the opposing myths we have about motherhood feed self-doubt and self-reproach.

Our society tends to look at mothers either as being flawless and loving, meeting all the expectations we have of them, or as being horrible and rejecting, meeting none of our expectations. They are one or the other, but nothing in between. We expect them to take perfect care of their families and to always be happy and patient. In this day and age, they are also often required to have a job outside of the home, thereby contributing to the economic well-being of the family. Mothers must operate in two very different worlds and do it all in a loving and selfless manner. (Of course, they're supposed to be thin and beautiful as they do all this!) Can anyone really be a perfect, all-loving being while anticipating and meeting all the needs of others and constantly communicating affection and support? We expect mothers to nurture us when we need it and back off when we don't; and, they have to know this without our telling them directly. Could any human being, man or woman, do all this? Who of us would be fool enough to sign up for such a job?

Women who choose a less traditional path, perhaps a single lifestyle, lesbianism, marriage without children, or a career-centered life, are not immune to this. Going against the family legacy or doing things differently from their mothers is not easy. It may be seen as a betrayal, thereby endangering the connections to the family. In these scenarios, parents, especially mothers, may ask what they "did wrong" that their daughters did not follow family tradition. Other relatives may criticize the parents as well. So, guilt sets in, both for the parents and for the young woman who is attempting to pave her own way in life—daring to follow her dreams.

Many young women do not see the guilt-provoking expectations for adult females as enticing. They may show their ambivalence by developing eating problems and denying their body's feminine nature. Feeling guilty about rejecting their mothers' lifestyle, they renounce themselves as well. They do not accept the myths that dictate women's roles, but they have no clear alternatives—the legacy of loyalty limits their vision and their experience. Their preoccupation with food and their bodies will distract them from this pain.

GRIEF

Mothers feel remorse for what they have done, but fathers reproach themselves for what they have not done. Thus, the father's emotional experience may be more similar to grief, the sharp sorrow or pained regret for how he has neglected others or has been neglected himself. Like guilt, grief is a shared experience in families who are loyal to the ill-fitting myths. Still, it more accurately describes the male experience, since his misgivings are about his absence and all the lost opportunities for him as a parent. Thus, while guilt may be the primary area to explore with women in therapy, grief represents "the doorway to a man's feelings."[2]

Why is grief such a common but difficult emotion for men? Once more we find the answer in the myths and traditions that compromise our emotional well-being. Earlier we discussed how little boys are rarely allowed to express feelings and are instead told to "keep a stiff upper lip." They grow up believing their feelings are wrong and that they should be dealt with as quickly as possible.[3] Furthermore, boys are pushed out of the nest by mother after a comfortable and often indulgent early life. All of a sudden, they are expected to act like big men. Although boys accept this cut-off from mom, they may always hope to find a similar connection. Their feelings of abandonment, repeated disappointment, and "no satisfaction" are a deep undercurrent that make men dread opening up emotionally, because they fear they will never regain control of themselves. Although they know they have years of pent-up losses and disappointments, they don't explore the sadness these have caused, and thus they leave their children vulnerable to the same painful cycle.

When a man who is unable to process his own sorrow and who feels inept as a parent confronts the strong emotions of adolescent daughters, he withdraws. If his daughter develops conflicts about food or her body, he may retreat even further into his core of grief. Although on the outside he appears to be hard and unfeeling, rational and calm, such men are often deeply affected internally by their daughters' problems. Unfortunately, their losses and their poor preparation for parenting paralyze them. They become stuck in a gridlock of grief.

Daughters in these families also experience loss and grief over their desire for a connection with dad. They may develop health-impairing or life-threatening problems in order to create an opportunity for their fathers to come to their rescue, or at least to be more involved in the family. Thus, severe eating problems may allow the father to overcome his past shortcomings and remorse. Often in therapy, families will need to explore the long-term origins of the father's grief, the sorrow he has felt over incomplete attachments with both men and women, and the regrets he has about his life. This process may be difficult for all involved (including the therapist) because it acknowledges that men have feelings counter to our expectations and world-view. However, the father's admission of his shortcomings, his feelings, his despair, and his concern for his family can be pivotal to his daughter's acceptance of her need for him.

ANGER

As with guilt and grief, anger does not belong exclusively to daughters. Parents will also feel it, particularly when facing the power and resiliency of the eating problems and body-image distortion, just as daughters will share their parents' guilt and sadness. But the emotions young women who develop eating and body-image problems have the most difficulty confronting are anger and rage.

Throughout modern history, the social roles and expectations for women have made anger the most unacceptable feeling for females. Today, young women handle their fury by obsessing about their bodies and food. These behaviors keep them from feeling much of anything. Anger becomes numbed by the anesthesia of eating, restricting, purging, exercising, or torturing their bodies in some other way.

Rarely can rage be identified under this torrent of symptoms. The problem for these young women is that they usually don't know they are angry, but therapists often describe them as "swallowing their anger." When I see the links between feeling misunderstood, unappreciated, ignored, or hurt, I try to help patients by justifying that anger would be a logical response. Sometimes I tell them they have "angerexia," not anorexia or bulimia.

The longer young women do not feed their bodies, the more their "angerexia" is fueled by the legacy of loyalty to old ways of living in families and in our culture. Rage grows when girls do not feel loved and cherished by their fathers, when they experience too many demands from mothers, when their own needs take second place, and when they perceive that their parents always expect them to be perfect. It is fertilized by a culture that constantly tells women how they should look, act, feel, and eat—a culture that changes these expectations to suit fashion trends and money-making motives rather than people's real needs. In this system, women's appetites for food, sex, and self-expression are censored, and bodies that are not skinny become indictments of poor character. These circumstances underlie angerexia.

Throughout these chapters, women have linked their eating problems and body-image dissatisfaction with anger. They are speaking, however, from the vantage point of recovery. During the height of their illness, most were unable to identify their rage. To recover, they had to uncover these feelings. Coming from families where they perceived shaky connections, constricted communication, and minimal expressions of love or affection, talking about such emotions was either not allowed or extremely risky. During recovery, daughters must be given permission and learn how to express their anger, just as mothers must manage their guilt and resentment, and fathers must experience their grief and responsibility.

LOSS

Families who experience extreme father hunger suffer feelings of great sorrow and loss. When their daughters develop eating problems, it may create an opportunity to explore and resolve the losses and to change future relationships. Still, the emotional damage can be gut-wrenching for fathers and mothers who were only trying "to do the right thing." Remember these are families that swallowed hook, line, and sinker the myths about men's and women's scripts. They firmly believed that following these cultural dictates and multigenerational patterns would assure their children's adjustment and happiness. So, along with the losses parents experience when their daughters develop conflicts about food and body-image is the breakdown of confidence in their parenting. They begin to question every decision they make and even to doubt their intentions of the past.

They also lose the shared fantasy that everything is perfect in their family. This is another severe injury to their sense of themselves as good parents. They know they'll have to find new ways to interact with their children and to be together, even though they believed they were on the right path, often hearing praise from others for their efforts. Both their self-esteem and their world view is shaken.

What's more, parents who spend time looking at their own families of origin, may uncover pain and disappointments that they had sealed over out of loyalty to tradition. Often, parents of young women with eating problems appear caught between their own parents and families of origin and their children. They rarely feel understood by their parents and may, in fact, feel criticized or undermined. They may experience much sadness as they begin the healing and change process.

ALIENATION

The sum total of the legacy of loyalty—compromised connections, divisions within the self, guilt, grief, anger, and loss—is alienation. Both the young woman, who expresses her confusion through food and her body, and her parents, experience this isolation and estrangement.

For the young woman, the total experience of the legacy of loyalty is one of being detached or separated from the world—both her inner reality and her interpersonal environment. She is cut off from her feelings, her body, her sense of self, her appetite, her femininity, her family, and her peers. She is also estranged from the culture into which she is supposed to assimilate.

Becoming part of the world outside the family and adopting the views, norms, and practices of the sociocultural environment is one of the critical tasks of adolescent and young adult development. A young woman who perceives she is not recognized, valued, seen, or heard by her father—in essence, not "real" to him, anticipates the same experience with the culture, for he is its most important representative. She wonders how she will ever become part of the world if she's not part of his life, and whether she will ever feel loved and accepted. She may decide that the best she can do is find a limited place for herself, one prescribed by the culture, not necessarily one of her choosing. So she does things that her father or the masculine system endorses; she expresses her femininity as endorsed and controls her impulses around food, her body, and her emotional needs. Hoping to connect to the world, she withdraws from herself; in reality she is cut off from everything. Her experience is alienation, and she feels estranged, alone, unaccepted, isolated, and confused.

Parents also share this sense of alienation when they involve themselves in their daughter's recovery. They feel cut off from their own parenting: the happiness they intended for their daughter has not materialized and they wonder what they did wrong. They question themselves endlessly, and they feel misunderstood by everyone—their daughter, friends, and families. They begin to question the values of a culture they have supported, and even the very lives they have lived. They ask themselves repeatedly: how could we have been so wrong?

Although the parents' alienation concerns their past, the daughter's revolves around the future. Her life is put on hold while she wrestles with how to become part of a world that feels hostile to women and one that has fed her father hunger. In the best of situations, families will confront and process these issues together. When parents, especially fathers, are willing to do this, they show their love in a very important way. They help their daughters to heal their father hunger and their food and body-image problems. With help from this special man, the daughters may discover how to become part of a dysfunctional culture without denying or destroying themselves.

THE PARENTS' PERSPECTIVE:
"We're still mourning all our losses, and I'm learning how to be a father. Neither of us really had one."

The following comments by parents of a young woman who had developed a serious eating disorder illustrate how these feelings of guilt, grief, anger, loss, and alienation flow from the legacy of loyalty to the myths about men's and women's roles in families. This couple was interviewed after a year of family therapy. While their daughter was on the road to recovery, they were still working hard to understand and change their patterns of interaction and to reverse the effects of father hunger in their lives.

Mother: What we went through as a family was really hard after Mary's problems developed. We read about eating disorders and we knew we needed to get into family therapy. But it was so scary.

Father: Our families had never been "talkers." We didn't realize how that had affected us, but we had been married for 25 years and we still didn't know how to communicate. I must admit I was worse than my wife—she was scared but I didn't even know how I felt. The therapist would ask questions and I would have no idea of what to say. Here I was, very successful, I owned my own public relations firm, and I couldn't even talk to my family.

Mother: Yeah, that was probably one of the biggest blows for both of us—we both had felt very successful. Sure, we worked hard, but it had paid off—all we ever heard from other people was that we had great kids—Mary especially got good grades and excelled at everything. We had never had any problems so we didn't know how to deal with them. When Mary got sick, I felt like my world had just been tipped upside down. Something was really wrong with us and with Mary, but I had no clue.

Father: And then you started blaming yourself for everything, remember? You felt so bad about yourself—so guilty. I would try to reason with you but it never helped. That's one thing I've learned—sometimes I'm too logical and don't give feelings enough air-time. I've gotten better, but I feel like I'm doing the opposite of what I was told to do all my life. Usually I feel better after I talk, but I must admit I'm not quite comfortable with it yet.

I think I actually was depressed my entire life—I just didn't know it. So I didn't always like the feelings I got in touch with.

Mother: You seemed so withdrawn and cold during that time. I needed emotional support because I felt so guilty, but you couldn't be there for me. That was another really hard experience. Now I think we know how to give each other room and emotional support. Back then I think we both felt alone. At least I did. I felt misunderstood by everyone. My daughter, my husband, my parents, my friends.

Father: I think we felt lots of losses. My wife is right—we didn't feel understood by anyone. Here we had done everything the way parents "should." My wife had read every book on child development ever written. We thought everything was perfect. Then our daughter develops this psychological problem that could kill her. Life will never be the same for me. I've lost my fantasy that we're the perfect family.

Mother: So there we were. Our daughter's in the hospital and we're in therapy trying to figure all this out. And we feel horrible about ourselves. And then, probably the biggest blow of all was how our parents handled it. We had always been very close to both sets of parents, and we felt completely let down. They couldn't deal with our not being perfect, I guess. We got no support from them. Here, we had lived our lives trying to please them. Now I know that was part of the problem—but they couldn't understand that we needed emotional support, that we needed to talk. We felt criticized and abandoned.

Father: I guess you could say we were caught between two generations. We were trying to change to help our daughter, but all we felt were the pressures and criticisms of our parents. They really don't understand and we've had to accept that. But it's caused us both a lot of sadness.

Mother: Maybe they're feeling guilty too? Maybe they're afraid to look at how they raised us. They were very traditional families. And they see us finding a new way to be together. I'm learning to speak more directly and ask my husband for help—he's much more involved as a father. Maybe it's a clash between the old and the new.

Father: What we know now is that the old ways didn't work for us, but we may not have even seen this if Mary hadn't developed these problems. One of the most important things I've learned is how Mary needs me—I can't leave all the parenting to my wife. I know I'm important to Mary. I also know how much my father missed because he was never close to me, and how much I missed as a son.

Mother: I missed a lot as a daughter, too. But we're working on things now. Somehow through our guilt and our sadness we'll make Mary's life better and help her in ways our parents couldn't. It's a different world so we're going to have to be different parents.

Father: Yeah, we've got to stop just trying "to do the right thing" and figure out what is right for us. I guess I'm still angry that although I was trying to do the right thing, to follow my family and what we all accepted, we all suffered so much. I've felt a lot of anger and frustration about things I can't control. Now I know how hard it is for girls to grow up surrounded by the media, the diet ads, the skinny bodies, and the focus on appearance. I had been oblivious to that—I just didn't know what was going on. I felt stupid for a while; now I feel outraged but I don't know what to do.

I guess you could say we're still mourning all our losses—as children and now as parents. Anger is only part of that. I'm learning how to be a father. Neither of us really had one. Our parents don't understand that at all, but I'm convinced my kids need me and I'm going to find a way to be there for Mary—and for me.

PART THREE

◆ ◆ ◆

THE SOLUTIONS TO FATHER HUNGER

CHAPTER 10

♦ ♦ ♦

HOW MEN CAN
OVERCOME FATHER HUNGER

In these next chapters, we look at what we all need to do to address the problems inherent in the contemporary father's role in the family. We start by examining what you as men can do to become more active parents and reverse the tradition and consequences of father hunger. The only thing that will counter the cynicism, disillusionment, and degradation surrounding fathers in our culture is for men to actively alter their behavior and become more emotionally available, expressive, and nurturing.

This chapter is designed to help you, fathers, to find ways to do this. With paternal love, daughters feel confident as they cope with their natural concerns about food, weight, body-image, and self-concept. Without it, they feel rejected by you and the culture you represent. Their resulting father hunger will cause them much agony and suffering.

Before you can become a more loving and available parent, however, you will have to face your own father hunger. For the first time you must connect to your feelings, instead of denying them. You will probably realize how you have separated from your disappointments about your dad and how this has not prepared you for being a parent, a spouse, or even a friend.

To begin this process, you must commit yourself to a psychological journey wherein you will experience parts of yourself and of life that have been blocked off because of the myths and traditions established for men in current western society. This new intimacy will be life-transforming, but frightening, because it will take you into uncharted, unfamiliar territory; it is, therefore, a heroic act. To be worthwhile, such a process must be gut-wrenching, provoking anxiety, self-doubt, and endless questions about your self-worth, your place in the world, and the values of our society.

History and mythology are full of examples of people who dared to embark on such adventures. The process always involves separation, initiation, and return, as described by Joseph Campbell:

> A hero ventures forth from the world of common day into a region of supernatural wonder: fabulous forces are there encountered and a decisive victory is won: the hero comes back from this mysterious adventure with the power to bestow boons on his fellow man.[1]

In other words, as you take this journey to become a more loving, involved father, your personal growth will isolate you at first and will turn you inward; but, you will eventually "return" as a new, enlightened man, capable of intimacy with yourself and with others. And you will be able to show your feelings, especially your love, to your daughter. This pilgrimage will teach you how to connect with others and how to feed your daughter's hunger with love.

Fathers who are struggling to understand their daughters' eating problems are already involved in such a mission. Your daughters' conflicts are challenging your sense of self, separating you from your tendency to live out the old myths about families, roles, and values, and preparing you to write new ones. Her condition has threatened, maybe even shattered, your concept of yourself as a father. I see the panic and desperation in your eyes when you first bring your daughter for therapy and realize that you haven't known the intense pain she was experiencing. I hear the anguish in your voice as you try to understand her distorted thinking about her body, and I sense the helplessness in your spirit when you can't make everything better for her. (After all, wasn't it always your job to solve the family problems?) I cannot guarantee that taking this heroic journey will assure your daughter's recovery. But I know that the more you examine yourself—your strengths and weaknesses as a father, a husband, and a man—and the more you explore your own father hunger, the more you will be emotionally available to your daughter.

As you change, your daughter will feel your love in a new way, and as you take your journey inward to understand and heal your wounds, you will be a great example to her of how to get to the emptiness underlying her eating problems. She also may feel less guilty for causing you to worry if she sees that you are becoming more involved and feeling more satisfied in your relationships. Acknowledging your own father hunger, the scars from your upbringing as a male, your estrangement from your own feelings, and your isolation, will eventually lead to new and gratifying connections to yourself, your world, and your ability to father.

FACE YOUR OWN FATHER HUNGER

Helping your daughter can only happen if you help yourself. To comprehend her experience as a child you must comprehend your own. To do this, you must reverse the years of experience wherein you discounted, denied, and thereby separated from your emotions. Now you must acknowledge and confront all the pain, hurt, disappointment, rejection, longing, and sadness you have had to ignore in order to be a "good boy" and a "real man." Chances are that you, like your daughter, grew up without intimacy in your relationship to your father—he was an elusive image, yet you desperately wanted to please and satisfy him and thereby feel connected to him. As a male, you could accomplish these things only by trying to be like him. Unfortunately, by imitating your father, you have repeated the pattern in your relationships with your children. To change this, you have to go back and feel what you ignored for so many years—you must face your own father hunger.

Connecting With Yourself

Those of you reading this book with the hopes of helping your daughters may not know where to begin. The answer is simple. Start with yourself. Take time to look inward and allow yourself to have feelings—all kinds, not just the easy ones. Tell yourself it's okay for men to be sad, to feel left out, to need others, to be angry for not getting true acceptance and unconditional love as you grew up. Break the rules you have been taught in the past; stop separating from your inner self and start connecting with it. Bring together the different parts of yourself, your underlying feelings with what you express through your behavior, and this will bring you and your daughter together. Separating from the old myths about men is essential as you try to develop new connections.

One of the most destructive beliefs we hold about men is that they don't feel. The fact is that men experience lots of strong emotions. Most of the time, however, you are expected not to show them. Instead, you are encouraged to "do," to achieve, thereby distracting you from this inner life. Your focus is on the outside, not the inside. As a result, your reflex is to tackle a problem rather than to experience it in an effort to get rid of anything and everything that causes discomfort or anxiety.

For your daughter's sake, and yours, allow yourself to feel, especially to be aware of the losses you have suffered. Don't fight the urge to cry or even to weep. Find some special trusted allies to support you through this. Some men develop informal networks of support with friends. Others form more structured men's groups that meet regularly, while still others choose to participate in organized spiritual retreats as they grapple with new means of expression.[2] By finding support in relationships with men, you can create the bonding you missed growing up and you can find proof that the old myths about men just aren't true. Most importantly, you can work through your own losses so they do not perpetuate themselves in your daughter's life.

At this point you need to become more conscious of the myths about men you have internalized. No doubt these are limiting your life in many ways and keeping you from being fully conscious of your feelings about your father. Most likely, you have ignored your own father hunger until recently. Consequently, you have not been able to actualize your potential as a parent and have been oblivious to how your children, especially your daughters, need you.

Take some time to review the myths about men—that you "can't understand," that you are insignificant to your children's development, that parenting is unimportant to you, that you don't feel, that your role is to provide economically, and that your daughters don't need you to grow up. You can choose to believe these and maintain the separateness you have been told to develop and value, or you can challenge them and become connected. If you decide to contradict the myths, your life will be fuller— attachments and connections will fill the old voids of your own hunger for closeness. Take this opportunity to actively decide which beliefs about men should guide your life, especially as a dad. Begin to pour the love you harbor into your relationships.

Questions and New Connections

- How did your father express feelings?
- How safe do you feel talking about feelings?
- What myths was your father demonstrating as you grew up?
- Of the myths about men, which ones bother you the most?
- Where can you find support and acceptance as you allow yourself to feel more?

Connecting With Your Father

To understand how your children feel or miss your love, you must go back in time to look at how you were fathered, and connect with your own father hunger. In a very useful book on the obstacles to paternal intimacy, Sam Osherson says this process necessitates, "healing the wounded father within, an angry-sad version of ourselves that feels unloved and unlovable."³ In other words, the scars men carry into adulthood from the distant, demanding relationship most have experienced with their fathers, have to be examined, treated, and healed. Pretending that they do not exist only prolongs the pain. Only with this insight and regeneration will men be able to father in a different way than they were fathered.

Gus Napier, a family therapist and author, describes the impact of fatherlessness on men who want to be more involved in their children's lives. He writes about his own deep wounds, "When men like me decide to try to be more involved fathers, we encounter this vast emptiness; we learn about the father who was not there."⁴

When you look at the relationship with your father, you will likely be shocked by your neediness. You were taught that you didn't need anything (other than money or "things") from him.

You may experience much pain when you realize that your life has been an attempt to cover up this emptiness and to maintain society's myths about men.

If your father is still alive, you should consider talking with him about the pressures he felt as a parent and the losses you felt as a son. If he is dead, you could instead talk to other relatives or family friends to gain insight into what motivated this mysterious man. Understanding more about his experience and why he was unavailable to you will help you avoid repeating the same mistakes.

Once you acknowledge your own father hunger, you will be more capable of understanding your daughter's experiences. Admitting how your father withheld love, affection, and acceptance and how you responded (through achievement, workaholism, denial, isolation) will lead you to find a different way to be a father. By exploring and then departing from your past, you will be renewed, capable of giving, loving, and understanding for the first time. Separating from the old ways will allow you to connect to the new.

Questions and New Connections

- What are some memories of your relationship with your father?
- How did he relate to you?
- What kept him from being a fuller, more loving father?
- What keeps you from this?

Finding Help in Therapy

Facing your father hunger does not mean repeating the pattern of handling things alone and needing no one. Seeking assistance from a therapist can help you overcome the tendency to separate and teach you how to connect. Sharing your feelings in therapy can be a turning point, because it can unlock many of the doors that the negative myths and roles for men have closed in your life.

Therapy, however, is a world different from the one for which men's socialization prepares them. Those who have a deep commitment to the outdated myths we've talked about throughout this book will generally have a hard time admitting they need the help of a professional's perspective. The scripts for fathers insist that you can take care of anything (the old "father knows best" syndrome)—but you can't! You will probably need guidance to switch gears, to learn how to question, not to answer, to explore issues, not to get rid of them. Therapy is the best way to start this process.

Working together in family therapy is an extremely effective way to get to know your daughter and to find ways to be more connected to her and the rest of the family. This closeness may not happen instantly, though. In fact, at first you may become aware of how much you haven't known about the emotional lives of other family members. You may feel uncomfortable and want life to go back to the way things were before all these emotions were being verbalized, or you may worry that all this talking is only going to cause more stress. You are tempted to jump into your role of protector, wanting to eliminate the problems. Although those old patterns may be familiar and secure, they contributed to your daughter's turmoil. Remember the old saying, "Sometimes things have to get worse before they get better." Often this is the case: what your daughter needs during this phase is to know that you love her, accept her, and respect her feelings, and that you will stand by her no matter how painful the issues or how long it takes to explore them together.

Sometimes people with eating problems resist their families' involvement in therapy, especially their fathers' participation. There are several possible reasons for this. You may be still focusing too much on her symptoms and not supporting her as a unique individual. Think about how to relate to her as a person, not just as your "anorexic" or "bulimic" daughter. She may also be afraid that you will be disappointed in her if she lets you know about her conflicts or insecurities. Furthermore, she may not trust your interest or affection; she may fear that your attention is temporary and that the only way to maintain it is for her to be sick. So, hang in there and you may gradually convince her of the permanence of your love.

Many fathers, once they overcome all the masculine barriers to seeking help, benefit from individual therapy also. Since your daughter's problems have shattered your identity as the protector and problem-solver, you need to rebuild your "self" as well. Looking back at your experience as a son, your expectations for fatherhood, and your own coping mechanisms, can be an invaluable way to improve your life. By supporting yourself with the assistance of a mental health professional, you will also be supporting your daughter. It can only help as you try to build a more satisfying and loving connection with her.

Although the notion and process of therapy runs counter to how you were raised, you may find it helpful and even fun! Fathers often tell me how they have enjoyed it. One expert in the treatment of men encourages them to become involved by using this analogy, "Being with a psychotherapist beats the hell out of being in a dentist's chair."[5] In fact, working with a therapist may be as essential to your well-being as your dental checkups.

Questions and New Connections

- How do you feel about therapy? What would your father think about it?
- What old myths keep you from seeking help from others?
- What issues do you need to work on to be more connected to your family?

WORK ON YOUR RELATIONSHIPS WITH WOMEN

In order to develop a nurturing and loving relationship with your daughter, you need to devote attention to how you relate to women in general. Your daughter has been watching your interactions with them for years, searching for clues about what you like about women and whether you value them. These impressions are very important to her as she moves toward womanhood. To understand her perceptions, you must examine your relationship with her mother, uncover how you are repeating your father's behaviors as a husband, and explore your attitudes and expectations about women. To correct some of your errors and revise your behavior so you can be more present to your daughter, you will have to figure out how to share power and responsibility with her mother, how to find a positive role for you in the family, and work together, even if you are divorced.

Connecting With Her Mother

One of the most important ways you can help your daughter is to look critically and honestly at your relationship with her mother. Family conflicts affect females very deeply. When girls are worried about their parents' happiness or marital stability, they don't have the emotional energy necessary to face the ups and downs of adolescence. Often, they will try to make things better for their parents and put themselves on hold. Men must address their relationships with their wives or ex-wives so their daughters can focus on their own needs, feelings, and desires.

By accepting that you may have flaws as a husband, you'll be a positive model for your daughter; your openness will convey that no one, even the most important man in her life, is perfect. In turn, this will help her overcome the constant struggles for perfectionism that her eating and body-image problems reflect. At the same time, you will also be emphasizing the importance you place on the relationship with her mother.

Take some time alone to work on this. Try to be honest about what kind of husband you have been. Resist the impulse to blame all the problems on your spouse. If you are willing to take an additional risk, ask her what she has experienced as your wife. As you proceed with this, it is essential that you find links between your experience in your family-of-origin and your style as a husband. Your abilities, strengths, deficits, and faults are probably direct consequences of the role your father had. If he was absent, aloof, or emotionally cut off, you did not learn how a man could express love and respect to his wife. If he didn't show you affection and didn't teach you how to love in his interactions with your mother, you are going to have to work hard to figure out how to have these in your marriage. You may not feel lovable nor be able to show love. By looking at how your father functioned as a husband and assessing how you have repeated his mistakes, you will be opening yourself up to a new way of relating and modelling this for your daughter.

For those of you who are separated or divorced, it is important that you own some of the blame for the breakdown of the marriage so that your daughter does not feel that the responsibility for relationships belongs only to women. Try to avoid discussing her mother's shortcomings (you probably have some too!) Your daughter needs to identify with the positive and loving parts of her mother as she becomes a woman. She probably already knows her mother's faults pretty well! She may have decided she has all the same traits as her mother or she may be trying to be completely different because of what she has observed in your interactions. Above all, resist the urge to put your daughter in the middle of your marriage or your divorce. Allow her the freedom to concentrate on herself, not on your problems.

Whether married, separated, or divorced, the messages fathers give daughters about their mothers are important. Essentially, if a father puts his wife down, he is also putting his daughter down, since the daughter's primary role model is her mother. Find out if your wife (or ex-wife) feels respected by you. If she doesn't, your daughter will not feel respected or secure either. Your connections with her mother will be the prototype of what your daughter expects to experience. Think about this; decide what you want her to have as a model and see if you can create it.

Questions and New Connections

- How am I similar to my father as a husband?
- How did my mother feel about their marriage?
- What patterns do I want to change?
- How could I improve my relationship with my wife (or ex-wife)?

Exploring Your Attitudes Toward Women

Your daughter will be keenly sensitive to your interactions with all women, not just your wife, so you need to be conscious of your beliefs and behaviors. It's likely that your notion of femininity is in transition, since women's roles have changed so much in recent decades. Take an inventory of your own attitudes toward women—what is femininity, what is the ideal woman, what do you want for your daughter, what do you value in women? By addressing these questions, you can become more aware of what your daughter may be absorbing from your behavior. Furthermore, you may realize that there are conflicts between what you say to your daughter and what you really mean.

As you work on this, try to remember how your father treated women when you were growing up. You may have internalized some of his attitudes unknowingly. By understanding these influences from your childhood, you can differentiate between what you want to convey to your daughter about being a woman and what you are unconsciously passing along from your family history.

Because of the differences between how you were raised and what life is like today, you are probably facing experiences you did not anticipate. For example, women have gained some power in the marketplace and men react to this in different ways. Some men resent women, while others respect them; some may have no trouble dealing with their newfound authority, but others will detest it. Many believe that women should not have certain kinds of jobs. Honestly explore these feelings, because they are going to be visible to your daughter.

Do you think that power and femininity co-exist, or do you believe that they cancel each other out? Consider how you want your daughter to integrate these qualities. Take time to think about the issues the women's movement has raised and how they are affecting your daughter. Discuss with her how women's roles and power have changed in your lifetime and how these shifts have affected your feelings around women and your interactions with her.

If you do not appreciate women and their concerns, your attitudes will be evident even if you give lip-service to more liberated notions. One test of whether you really value women and take your daughter seriously as a separate young person with her own ideas and feelings is very simple. It has to do with listening.

Often, fathers discount their daughters' worries instead of listening to them. For example, when your daughter tells you she is worried about her math grade, a typical response is: "Don't' worry, with your great smile, no one will ever notice if you need a calculator to balance your checkbook." Although you intended to be supportive, you did not listen to her. Instead, you filtered the issue through your own notions of feminine behavior—you have just said that her smile and her appearance are more important than her feelings or her sense of competence. She will wonder if she should take herself seriously, since you don't. So, be sure to say what you mean.

Another way to determine your attitudes toward women is to compare how you approach boys and girls. You would probably give your son different advice about math by clearly stating that math is important and he needs to study. You should treat your daughter with the same respect and take her concerns seriously. Furthermore, you should give both sexes equal opportunities to develop themselves, even if your daughter is interested in areas that are not traditionally feminine. In these ways, you communicate support and recognition of her as a female with legitimate rights, feelings, and desires. Your actions will have told her that, as is, she is acceptable to you and worthy of your love and that women are equal to men.

Carefully listen to yourself to detect any potentially negative attitudes toward women or toward your daughter that you might convey in your jokes, lectures, or off-hand remarks. Also, you should tune into your daughter's reactions to you, for she may pick up messages you don't wish to give her. Better fathering requires that you examine your attitudes toward women to be sure that these do not inadvertently jeopardize your daughter's development and sense of self.

Questions and New Connections

- How are my attitudes toward women similar to my father's?
- What beliefs about women do I want to convey to my daughter?
- Do I listen to my daughter? Does she feel that I listen to her?

Rearranging Roles in the Family

If your daughter is waging war with food and with her body, she is struggling to gain power. She has no other vehicle for autonomy and effectiveness in the world because she has not seen a more appropriate way to exert control and share authority in relationships. Daughters growing up in a culture with unhealthy, imbalanced power distributions need you, their fathers, to try to understand and correct these patterns. You may not appreciate how confusing power is to your daughter unless you examine how you own and express it at home.

Although the cultural conflicts men and women have about power are not of your making, you still need to look at how you personally are contributing to your daughter's turmoil about how to find it. Consider if you approach family interactions with an old, internalized picture of father left over from your childhood. If your family treated him as the ultimate authority—"king of the castle"—you probably experience difficulty knowing how to share authority with your wife. Although fathers who come out of the shadows sporadically to take charge have great influence in a family, this kind of authority is paradoxical because it is based on absence, not presence. Your dad was probably lonely and unsatisfied. His power did not bring him love or intimacy. If you want these things, you have to act differently.

To this day, women maintain power in the family because they have responsibility for the home, for food, for the emotions and health of the family, and for child-care. Even in families in which both parents work, mothers still provide two thirds of the child-care. Fathers tend to do the more pleasant child care tasks, like taking the kids to the park so mom can clean the house, do the grocery shopping, or run errands. In single-career homes where wives work as full-time homemakers, fathers spend less than one fourth of the time mothers spend interacting with the children.

Although fathers in dual-career couples devote more time to the children, they still assume little responsibility for the nuts and bolts of child-rearing.[6] In both cases, children get disproportionately more of mom and less of dad. As a result, families remain deprived of a father. Mothers over-function, fathers under-function, and their daughters learn how to repeat this pattern instead of how to take care of themselves.

Examine the day-to-day activities in your home and figure out what you can do to function more fully as a parent. Look carefully at the distribution of duties between you and your wife. You might keep track of who does what over a period of a few days or a week. You probably will find that she does much more than you. Try doing some of the things your wife does instead of the peripheral tasks most fathers do. Talk to her about how you could operate more equally in the daily life of the family. This will show her that men and women share responsibility for relationships.

Once you have reassigned household tasks, look at the power distribution in your family. Work with her mother to provide a model of shared parental control, decision-making, and responsibility. This will assure your daughter that there are other ways to feel capable and effective, that she needn't deny herself food or attain a perfect body to gain your respect.

Questions and New Connections

- What kind of power do you hold in the family?
  How does your wife (or ex-wife) have power?
- How are decisions made in your family?
- Are there some jobs at home you absolutely view
  as women's work and refuse to do?
  What are they and why?
- In your daily life at home, how similar are you to
  your father?

Coping With Divorce

Your crusade to find a more fulfilling role as a father is apt to be much more difficult if you are divorced or living separately from your daughter. In these circumstances, many factors affect the father-child relationship, including remarriage, geographic distance, custody arrangements, visitation rights, and the children's developmental issues. Divorce does not have to destroy your relationship with your daughter. Still, if you try to play an active role as a divorced father, you are defying a number of the myths you were taught. You may need assistance to figure out how to have this different kind of life. Again, therapy will help, but so will talking and listening to your daughter.

The importance of parents' working together and fathers being active and available in their daughters' lives does not evaporate when a marriage dissolves. Although some divorced couples find mutually agreeable ways to share custody and time with their children, most are unable to work together to co-parent their children. The myths that mothers are instinctively better parents and that fathers are inept lead many men to abdicate their parenting role. Once more, mothers end up with sole responsibility for the children. In turn, this may lead to the mother's feeling bitter and resisting any involvement of the father in the children's lives. Children lose the opportunity to have two active, caring parents.

Look at the following divorce statistics and think about their implications. Today, up to 50% of new marriages end in divorce and 90% of the children are in sole custody of their mothers.[7] By early adolescence, 50% of American children in these families have no contact with their fathers; 30% have sporadic contact, only 20% see their fathers weekly or more frequently.[8] More than 11 million children in the United States have less than daily contact with their fathers.[9]

Before you continue reading, look at the statistics again. Actively decide if you want to be part of them. Remember, 80% of children of divorce have little or no contact with their dads! To avoid this, start addressing your relationship with your ex-wife and listening to your children. Use the crisis of your divorce to reassess the roles you want to have.

In some cases, divorce actually improves a father's relationship with his children. For one thing, it may end the constant tension or fights between parents, and for another, it may leave you more emotionally available to your children. Until you have adjusted to your new lifestyle, the transition period can be very painful, but at the same time it may give you the opportunity to develop a relationship with your children without always having your wife in the middle. You should plan to be available to them regularly because they probably need to see you more, not less. Although you may be tempted to work longer hours to earn more money or to provide a new structure to your life now that you're alone, keep in mind Liz's words, "All I wanted was my father's love." A divorce disrupts your lives but it does not have to disrupt your love.

Questions and New Connections

- How can you divorce your wife but not divorce your children?
- How is their mother in the middle of the relationships with your children?
- How could you spend more time with your children?

HELP YOUR DAUGHTER TO SATISFY HER FATHER HUNGER

Once you have begun to face your own losses and wounds as a son and to address your relationships with women, you are ready for the next step in overcoming father hunger. Helping your daughter to manage her disappointments with you and other men, to assert herself in relationships, to feel valued as a unique individual and as a woman, are lofty goals. To reach them, you will have to build a stronger basis to your relationship by learning how to be a fuller, more present father, and by responding to her developmental needs and changes. This requires listening to her and assessing your own attitudes about food, weight, and body-image to determine how these may have affected her. It also necessitates finding ways to cope with her eating problems and to support her treatment.

Connecting With Your Daughter

Having a close relationship with someone else, even with your own flesh and blood, should be easy, but it isn't for most men. The constant pressure to separate and handle things independently and to avoid feelings affects every aspect of a man's life. Even the most powerful human experiences and the closest attachments are sifted through this ingrained way of looking at life. For most of you, to enjoy a close relationship with your daughter will require much self-examination and willingness to change.

Since relationships, feedback, and approval are important to your daughter, try to be more involved and more present at home. Praise and reinforce her so she knows she's good enough for you, that she has satisfied you. As you talk to her, get away from the tendency to present yourself as all-knowing and all-powerful. Let her know that everyone has worries and self-doubt, that no one is perfect, and that you are human. If she sees you in these new ways, she may be able to control the perfectionistic impulses that cover up her lack of self-acceptance and her constant attempts to satisfy you. If she already has your attention and affection, she won't have to do anything self-destructive to get it.

If you share more of your thoughts and feelings with your daughter, you will be less of a mystery to her, and the world of men will not be so frightening. Equipped with knowledge about what motivates, bothers, or pleases you, she will feel more comfortable with the opposite sex, less anxious about whether she will be able to function or find happiness in the world outside the family, and more confident of herself overall. She won't have to cope with the insecurity and self-doubt that can overwhelm young women and result in their denying or destroying their bodies through disordered eating. The more you reveal yourself to her, the more your masculine world will seem inviting rather than intimidating.

Similarly, the more interest you show in your daughter, the more she will believe that men respect and value women. If she is struggling with her body-image and eating, she needs to know that you are interested in her as a whole person. Avoid the tendency to focus on your worries about her symptoms, as it reinforces her beliefs that weight and food intake are the most important parts of herself. Build a broader basis to your relationship, so she in turn will become aware of her other qualities. Be sure to discuss values, beliefs, community issues, relationships, emotions, and problems in a give-and-take manner. Express your ideas but ask to hear hers in return. Show tolerance and acceptance if you differ. Most of all, convey respect and caring for her as a person, not just as an obedient daughter.

Questions and New Connections

- How well do you know your daughter as a person?
- How well does she know you?
- How could you get to know her better?

Learning To Listen

To find a more positive role for yourself in the family and to help your daughter define herself, you must learn how to listen. This may sound elementary, but it is not. You have grown up being told to be independent and separate, so you may not have skills for developing connections and interdependence. Not only does listening foster connection but it also is one of the most important gifts you can give your daughter, because it conveys trust and faith in her judgments, thereby empowering her. These are pivotal building blocks to self-esteem and self-concept.

Listening is very different from lecturing, but you may confuse the two. As a man, you often are in a position of authority at work and believe that you are supposed to be the expert at home as well. Lecturing may be second nature to you; it's just part of your role as problem-solver. One way to check the quality of your communication with your daughter is to consider how it resembles the way you approach subordinates at work. The more similar it is, the less appropriate it is to your relationship with your daughter. Remember, she's not an employee; she's your daughter and she's struggling to become an adult and leave her childhood relationship with you behind. She needs your respect and support, not your domination. As you switch roles from your public role in the community and workplace to your private role as father, you need to communicate in a different way. Basically, you need to disclose more of yourself emotionally and to listen more.

Listening empowers, while pep talks and lectures disempower. To your daughter, they may just be further indications of how out-of-sync the two of you are. To help her, you need to connect with her pain and accept her where she is emotionally. You probably can remember the frequent refrain you heard from your parents as a kid: "That doesn't hurt." (In fact, that toothache, bee sting, or scraped knee did hurt, didn't it?) To her, your pep talks may feel a lot like "that doesn't hurt." So be careful—you could be doing more harm than good. Leave the lectures at the office and switch to real communication—disclosing yourself and listening to others—at home. Family therapy can help. You may learn a great deal by watching how the therapist approaches your daughter. Gradually you will recognize when your daughter would like a pep talk and when she doesn't. On your own, it may be very difficult to know when she needs what from you.

Fathers often convey a strong belief that any obstacle can be overcome by sheer will power. Be careful not to go overboard with these positive messages. You may inadvertently convey that recovery is another arena where she must perform to earn your love. Quite likely, she will feel increased pressure to please you, a pattern she is trying to change. But, fearing she can't recover "perfectly," she may give up. Being lectured also activates the conflicts she has about whether she is living her own life or only living to please others. Recovery, therefore, becomes one more task to do for others—an extension of her selflessness. In reality, it must be based on desires that come from within her: she has to feel she is worthwhile and that she alone owns and is responsible for her body and her life. Encouraging your daughter to articulate how she really feels and to recognize the disappointments she has suffered will be more valuable than your lectures or pep talks.

The gift of listening that you offer your daughter will also open up your awareness and enrich your life. Try it!

Questions and New Connections

- Remember an occasion of your own when you felt truly heard. What was this like?
- What was it like to talk to your father?
- How do you want your daughter's experience to be different?

Redefining Fathering

Your concept of being a father should be an organic, flexible one. More than likely, this notion is different from what your father's life conveyed. What children needed (and often did not get) 30 years ago, and what children need today, are not the same. Furthermore, your daughter's desires will be distinct from yours because of the unique experiences children of each sex have as they grow up. Also, what your daughter needed from you when she was five is not the same as what she requires at the age of fifteen. So you must commit yourself not to specific behaviors, but to a way of being a father that responds to your daughter's development and to the differences between her feminine urge to maintain connections and your masculine emphasis on separateness.

One way to begin to redefine fatherhood is to imagine new myths for fathers that will replace the old ones we have discussed throughout this book. Look at your day-to-day interactions at home, paying close attention to how available you are on a feeling level. You might keep a journal and every night write how you shared your emotions with your daughter and whether you were behaving according to the old myths or following your new ones. Analyze how well you listened to her that day as well, since that's also going to need time and practice.

As you try to establish a closer relationship with your daughter, be sure to observe her need to gradually grow away from you and the security of home. You may want to recreate what you both have missed as she was growing up. You may actually want more closeness with her than she can deliver, because of her natural developmental progression away from the family, toward other relationships. Consciously try to let go of the little girl you cherished and allow her to become a woman. For her to feel comfortable as an adult, she needs you to accept her as one. Talking with other fathers will give you insights on how other fathers have dealt with their feelings as their daughters matured. In the end, you will have had a much fuller life if you allow your definitions of fathering to be dynamic and in transition.

Questions and New Connections

- What is the ideal father like today?
- How different was your father from this?
- How different are you?

Checking Your Beliefs about
Food, Weight, and Body-Image

Fathers of daughters who are conflicted about food and body image also need to examine their beliefs and behaviors related to food, weight management, and exercise. Earlier we examined how troubling these subjects are for women, but today men are also becoming concerned about them. The messages you receive about these issues, however, generally relate to being strong and healthy, living a long life, and avoiding cardiovascular disease. The messages women receive concentrate mostly on appearance.

Therein lies an important difference: women endanger their lives to be thin, while men believe that being thin will prolong their lives. Both of you have absorbed erroneous or conflicting information to support these views; part of your work as a father requires that you look more objectively at your own beliefs and behaviors around food and body-image.

You may need to educate yourself about the connections between nutrition, weight maintenance, and health. In their messages to men, food, dieting and exercise industries are promoting the notion that lower weight leads to a longer life. They are often distort or exaggerate the potential negative effects of higher weights.

Higher weights are not necessarily correlated with earlier death. Research does not show a direct connection between weight and cardiovascular disease, hypertension, diabetes, or other conditions that the diet industry lists as they try to drum up business. Repeated studies indicate that extreme obesity and extreme thinness are linked to mortality, but most data suggest that optimal weight is at or above the average for both sexes.[10] The Metropolitan Life Insurance Company issues a table of desirable weights based on actuarial studies of longevity and health that are accepted standards in the United States. Recently they revised the guidelines upward, indicating that higher weights are not clearly linked to medical problems or early death.[11] Because men want to be productive and take care of their families, however, the messages that link weight to health and longevity are very powerful. As a result, many men reading this book may have their own hang-ups or misguided notions about weight and food and these may have affected their daughters' beliefs.

In many families I have treated, the fathers were dissatisfied with their bodies and wanted to lose or control their weight. Their daughters were keenly aware of the fathers' concerns about weight, diet, and exercise, and often tried to help them by developing exercise programs, working out with them, and cooking low-calorie meals. These young women attempted to be a healthy model or to please dad through their own successful weight-loss or exercise programs.

Educating yourself about our culturally-accepted biases concerning weight and body-size can help. You may be influenced by weightism, a prevalent prejudice against large people in our society. You may have said many negative things about fat people to your daughter. She may be trying to assure your love by controlling her appetite and being thin. Think about what you have communicated to her about the connection between your love and people's bodies. Examine how important a person's size and appearance are to you. Be honest with yourself about whether you trust, like, or respect thin people more than fat people. Think about how weight and sex appeal interact in your reactions to women. You may believe that you can't love a fat woman. Consider what you have communicated about her mother's body due to these attitudes.

These are important questions because your daughter treasures and respects your opinions and wants to please you. Conceptualize how eating, weight, body shape, and fat may have become entangled into her perceptions of your love for her. Take time to figure out how you feel about these issues and what you really want to convey to her.

Questions and New Connections

- How important is appearance and weight to you?
- How are your feelings about a woman affected by her weight?
- How do you feel about your daughter's weight?

Coping With the Eating Problems

Anorexia, bulimia, yo-yo dieting, and compulsive overeating are especially hard to overcome because food is an absolute necessity of life. The person with conflicts about eating must face the problematic substance many times every day, every time food is planned, prepared, consumed, and cleaned up. So the family must find a way to manage food in the house while structuring it in a helpful way for the person who has the most difficulty with it. Who shops, who cooks, who cleans up, who eats together, can become major issues. It's important for the father to be part of the solution to these issues—they should not become the sole burden of his wife.

Again, your own childhood issues may affect how you handle your daughter's eating behaviors. You may believe that since you're the father, she should just do what you say, even when it comes to eating. So, instead of tuning into how *she feels* about food and trying to comprehend her pain, you simplify the problem and tell her, "Just eat normally." She will not feel loved if you nag about her eating. Instead, she will feel let down, misunderstood, and alone. If she experiences a twinge of anger, she will soon feel guilty and then will have even more trouble with food. The more you try to take over, the more you will wreak havoc.

Take a minute right now to imagine what it must be like to be so petrified of food, so worried about every mouthful, and so dominated by it. Imagine the pain and agony that your daughter suffers. Let her know that she can talk to you about it when she wants or needs to and that you will support her and love her no matter what. Ask her if you can help in any way. Most importantly, accept that these odd behaviors around food are actually illnesses and do not take it personally if she refuses your logic or your willingness to help.

If you find yourself getting angry, again remind yourself that she has an illness—she is not in complete control. You can help your daughter simply by trying to get to know her as a person and by showing her respect. Her symptoms, especially her eating, may be distracting, so you will have to work hard to counteract this.

The more you focus on her symptoms, the more you reinforce that her body-image and eating are the most important things about her. You reinforce this single-mindedness with questions such as, "What's your weight?" or "Did you throw up today?" Furthermore, if you talk to her only about her problems, she may feel her symptoms are the only way to get your attention and will be reluctant to give them up.

You need to build a bigger base to the relationship between you and your daughter. This does not mean that you should go to the other extreme and ignore her problems. That is even more dangerous; either she may feel you do not care at all or your denial could intensify her own. She may believe she can never get your love or attention, or she might take more drastic measures to get it (losing more weight, vomiting more, or hurting herself in another way). You might want to solve her problems by taking over, or you may succumb to your tendency to disconnect from difficult emotional situations. Try to find a middle ground. Let her know that you care, that you will help if she wants this, and that you love her despite these problems no matter how long her recovery may take.

Questions and New Connections

- What would your father do if his daughter had eating problems? How did he respond to problems in general?
- How are your responses similar to or different from his?
- In what ways does your daughter need you as she tries to recover?

Supporting Your Daughter in Treatment

The treatment process for people with eating problems is long-term, with slow, small steps. Even after the individual has changed her behaviors around food and her body, she needs help to understand how to deal with life's disappointments and challenges without hurting herself. This is best accomplished through relationships with a therapist, dietitian, and other health-care professionals. These connections promote the healing.

Fathers, with their years of listening to masculine messages like "you can do it on your own," "go for it," or "beat it," do not instinctively understand the nature of the treatment or recovery process. You must accept that both you and your daughter need help. Abandon all your old "macho" notions and replace your "I-don't-need-anybody" and "I-can-do-anything-I-put-my-mind-to" beliefs with ones that will allow your daughter to connect to the people who can help her. You must acknowledge that you need guidance and direction from others. If you admit this, it will be easier for your daughter to engage in treatment. Otherwise, she will feel that you disapprove of her and see her as weak or disloyal to you.

Once you have taken the major step of seeking help and allowing professionals to become part of your life, you must adjust your impatience and desire for instant results to the pace of your daughter's recovery. You will likely feel that no progress is being made because you don't intuitively understand what recovery involves and may not see her internal changes or the small adjustments she's making with her eating. While it is certainly okay for you to share your doubts, be careful how you do this. Otherwise, she will feel once more that she is disappointing you, that you can't accept or love her, that you will never understand.

You may have further difficulty accepting the pace of recovery because of your background and expectations. Try to get away from the masculine way of seeing the world and solving problems. Recovery is a more feminine process, based on uncovering the pain your daughter has felt when she was disconnected from you, her mom, the rest of the family, her peers, and the world. It requires making new, fuller, healthier connections. So blend this awareness of the need for connectedness into your psyche. Allow her the time to make these new connections and allow her the opportunity to connect with you.

Patience is probably the quality fathers have to work on the most. You must be patient with her recovery from her symptoms and with her ability to relate to you. Sometimes a father is more ready than his daughter to rebuild their relationship. Because she is working hard in so many areas to recover, and because she is at a different developmental point than you, she may need to address many other issues or attachments first. She will gradually get to you if you can wait. If you put pressure on her to work out your relationship before she's ready, she may feel scared by the intensity of your needs or she may, once more, feel out of control of her life. Be patient—having a better connection with her will be worth it!

Questions and New Connections

- What kind of messages have you been giving your daughter about treatment?
- What do you hope will result from her treatment?
- What recovery timetable is comfortable for you?
- What do you think is your daughter's timetable?

Your journey has just begun. I hope, as Campbell suggests, that it will be full of "fabulous forces" and that your "decisive victory" will be one of love—loving your daughter more freely because you have begun healing the wounds left by your own father hunger. The changes you must make as you overcome your separateness and become connected to yourself, to other men, to women, and especially to your daughter, may seem insurmountable. However, if you start with the right equipment—support from your family, friends, and therapists—eventually you will be able to feed your daughter and fill her father hunger with your love.

CHAPTER 11

◆ ◆ ◆

HOW MOTHERS CAN HELP

Men and women must share the challenge of overcoming father hunger and transforming roles in families to adjust to the realities of life as we approach the 21st century. Many women reading this may think: "Why do I have to change again? I've been changing for the last 20 years!" They have been working hard to expand their lives and pursue new opportunities brought on by the feminist movement. However, this next series of changes could bring a much more satisfying balance between the sexes. Because of the private power they hold in families, women can do a great deal to help daughters connect with fathers and to help men to overcome their separateness. The rewards could be sweet.

Just as men have to take a journey inward to become more active, loving, and available fathers, women must also engage in a process of transformation that includes exploring how father hunger has affected their personal development, identity, and skills as a wife and parent. Fathers have to learn how to connect and mothers have to learn how to separate, feel less responsible, and find balance between self and other. In this way, working on your own issues will equip you to support your daughter through recovery.

FACING YOUR OWN FATHER HUNGER

Father hunger is not something just your daughter and her generation experience; you suffered it as well. The two of you may be on parallel tracks; consequently, she will handle hers better if you pave the way by understanding and managing your own. The first step in your journey is to feel your own father hunger. Until now, you have probably denied these feelings and have been unaware of how they have affected your self-esteem, identity, goals, values, relationships, marriage, parenting, and life-decisions. Get ready to be shocked by the power of these new discoveries—anything that has been avoided for so long is going to be scary and disruptive. Your father may have played out his cultural role quite well, so in that way he was a model or prototype, but you will probably find that he wasn't ideal to you emotionally. That realization will hurt. Facing reality often does.

Your Family Legacy

To understand the residual effects of your father hunger, begin by tracing the outline of your father's imprint on your life. Think back to your earliest memories of him and the feelings between the two of you. Be honest about how much you tried to please him and whether you ever felt you accomplished this. Try to recall how your relationship changed as you got older. You may have felt connected to him at some points but not at others. Remember what you did to try to develop more of a bond between the two of you. The most basic issue is how satisfied you felt in the relationship. Take time to ponder that.

You may have limited your life to get your father's approval or you may have surpassed his expectations for the same reason. Consider how his values and beliefs affected your decisions. He may have seen certain jobs, hobbies, or activities as appropriate only for men. Figure out how these attitudes affected your participation in school, sports, and hobbies, your career aspirations, and how they still impact your decisions. Your father hunger has also influenced your choices in relationships, especially the types of men you are attracted to and the way you act around them. You need to detect how your behavior and expectations as a woman, a wife, and a mother reflect the interpersonal history between you and your father.

Once you have explored these patterns, you will understand firsthand how a father can affect a daughter's feelings about herself. It's natural to feel sad, let-down, even bewildered that you hadn't recognized this before. Eventually the pain will subside but only after you have faced it. To heal your own father hunger, you must learn how to separate from his expectations and the influence he still has on your behavior and emotions. You can survive in a healthier, more balanced, and more self-generated style than you have up to this point. In turn, your daughter will learn how she can address issues with her father.

As you discover more about how your relationship with your father affected you as a woman and now as a parent, you may want to share this with your daughter. Be sure to acknowledge that your experiences are different and that you each have to find your own solutions. Give her the message that you believe in her, so she will feel confident about solving the dilemmas she confronts in life, beginning with the relationship with her dad.

Questions and New Connections

- Have you ever felt comfortable and satisfied in your relationship with your father?
- How have you tried to get his approval?
- How do your adult interactions, especially with men, reflect your relationship with your dad?

The Delicate Balance: Self versus Other

For you to feel entitled to a mature, loving relationship with your dad, you must first strengthen and develop your own sense of self. Your work is different from what I prescribed for fathers, which was to connect to others. As women, you already are good at that. Now you need to be comfortable focusing on yourself and being more separate, both from your father's needs or expectations and from your daughter's disappointments with her dad. This new attention to self means that you must depart from the emotional aftermath of your father hunger and discover new ways to function in all your relationships.

Think about the constant conflicts you experience between pleasing others and expressing your own needs. More than likely, you often feel forced to choose between self and relationships, because your upbringing emphasized devotion to caretaking and nurturing, especially of men. Just like stockbrokers handle other people's money, you handle other people's feelings. You are at risk for "de-selfing," since these patterns can lead you to "betray and sacrifice the self in order to preserve harmony with others."[1] Think back to your early relationship with your father and honestly assess how much room there was for your needs. More than likely, in those interactions you were de-selfed, trying to connect any way you could, hoping to win his love and attention.

For women, de-selfing results in a dangerous pattern whereby too much of the self is negotiable. "We" becomes far more important than "I." Thus, the early relationship with dad can establish a standard of selflessness that lasts a lifetime and is an unhealthy model for your daughter. You can reverse the years of "de-selfing" and re-self, only by departing from the past. Once you do this, you will have a stronger identity, you will be able to deal with your own father hunger and your daughter's with a fresh perspective.

Questions and New Connections

• How do you balance your needs with those of others?

• What or who comes first in your life?

• How can you find more room for your "self" in your life?

Learning How To Be Angry

Women expend tremendous amounts of energy riding the waves of anger. Unexpressed rage comes out in other ways and contributes to depression in adult women and to many problems in marriages. Their inability to deal with this emotion emanates from a cultural expectation that was learned as a child: quite simply, girls are not supposed to be angry. Expressing anger, especially to or about your father, was forbidden.

Most women are aware of this unwritten rule about anger, so they continually question its legitimacy, and fear it. Although it's acceptable for a man to express it, if a woman does, she is seen as "a real turn-off," "unattractive," "masculine." Annoyance or irritation are not considered attractive or feminine. In many instances, the only time women express anger is when they are extremely irate, maybe even hysterical. This is not the right climate for working through feelings or understanding what needs to change. If you do not express your anger, you are not really communicating.

The very first step to helping you and your daughter with emotional expression is to reconsider your beliefs about anger. Instead of viewing it as problematic and destructive, look at it as a vehicle that will enhance your "self" and be constructive to your relationships. Begin to put your anger into words.

The Dance of Anger by Harriet Goldhor-Lerner[2] is a masterful book that shows how unresolved anger can create deep, dark shadows in our lives. It also shows how working through it can create important changes in your life. Anger can be a positive force, or as Lerner states, "Anger is a tool for change when it challenges us to become more of an expert on the self and less of an expert on others."[3]

This does not mean that venting anger will solve everything. In fact, just expressing your rage may serve to maintain the old patterns. Instead, you have to work to understand why you're so angry and to know what you can do to effect change. Trace it back to your relationship with your father. Look at how you handled anger with him and whether you ever expressed it directly. Think about how these feelings have surfaced in other areas of your life. For example, ask yourself how much you deny these feelings to maintain connections with the opposite sex. Honestly assess how your problems with anger reflect your tendency to please everyone else and deny yourself.

Women with eating problems show their struggles with self-worth and their rage through their bodies. Compulsive eaters are said to be swallowing their feelings, bulimics throw them up, and anorexics completely deny them. Feeling worthy of anger and feeling strong enough about oneself to express it are major steps toward recovery because they re-balance the self/other tensions. Your work in this area will help your daughter also to feel entitled to her anger and to find symmetry and equality in her relationships.

Questions and New Connections

- Did you ever express anger to your father? How? How did he react?
- What happened when you openly disagreed with him?
- What are you teaching your daughter about anger?

Using Your I-Voice

To find more balance between your self and others requires that you learn how to recognize and utilize your feelings to promote your own separate development. As you build a stronger personal identity, you will actually find more pleasure in relationships. So, working on your self-development also addresses your self-in-relationship. Paying attention to your communication style may help you become more assertive and expressive.

You need to develop a voice that will speak from the "self" to your significant others. Instead of the old blaming refrains that begin with "You" cultivate a voice that speaks with "I." The I-voice is assertive and more powerful and will get you closer to resolution of a problem in a way that blaming never does. For example, your husband is more likely to listen to you if you say, "I really feel insecure about our relationship when we spend so little time together" than if you say, "You don't love me. You'd rather work than be with me."

Think about how your relationship with your dad would have been different if you had been able to speak in an I-voice as a little girl. You might have said, "Daddy, I need you to tell me you love me," instead of guessing how to make him happy and hoping he cares. This would have affected your relationships with men throughout your lifetime. You would have known how to connect with men without giving up yourself. You still can learn this if you are willing to work at it.

As you develop your I-voice, you may find that some of those old myths about men (especially that men don't feel and men just can't understand) get in the way. You have to challenge and discard them, for they keep you from speaking directly and getting your needs met in relationships. They feed your de-selfing tendencies, so you give up easily and never learn to speak in the I-voice. You'll be able to leave your father hunger behind only when you are more grounded in yourself. Practice with your I-voice to express your disappointments and needs, especially to men. Don't let the eternal desire to please and to be connected to your father keep you disconnected from your own self.

Questions and New Connections

- How did your parents discourage your I-voice?
- What are some important I-voice statements that you would like to have said during your childhood?
- How are you discouraging or encouraging your daughter's I-voice?

Formulating Goals

To achieve the elusive equanimity between self and other, between separateness and connectedness, women have to formulate their personal goals and then stick to them. By bringing your father hunger into consciousness, you can now decide how much you will allow it to continue to dominate you. You can assess whether trying to please men to make up for your dad's indifference should continue to rule your life. Once you grapple with this, many other decisions become easier. You may, for instance, decide that you no longer have to dress a certain way or diet to maintain a weight that pleases men, but starves you. Perhaps you'll set more realistic goals for yourself in terms of work, community involvement, or even housekeeping. Whatever the area, dealing with your father hunger will free you to set priorities and follow them. This will be an extremely effective model for your daughter.

Take some time to think about what you want out of life right now. List the most important feelings you want to have. Look at how your tendency to focus on others, your self-denial, and your longing to please men have gotten in the way of these. Stop worrying so much about everyone else's happiness and start concentrating on your own. This will gradually allow you to be both separate from the demands of others and connected to yourself in your relationships. Initially, just thinking about your own desires may seem foreign, but breaking this new ground will create new opportunities for your daughter as well. Instead of obsessing about how to please her father and other men, she may follow your lead and develop goals of her own.

Questions and New Connections

- How do your goals reflect or contradict your father's goals for you?
- What obstacles have kept you from reaching your goals?
- Do you allow your daughter to develop and pursue her own goals?

Dealing with Your Guilt, Feelings of Failure, and Perfectionism

Guilt and responsibility seem to come with the territory of motherhood and are reinforced by the countless pages in books and articles devoted to the mother-child relationship. They are also fed by father hunger; always trying to do more, attain perfection, and please others become habitual responses.

Mothers of children with eating problems feel more than their share of these agonizing emotions. Usually by the time I first meet the mother of a new patient, the mother has read at least five books about eating disorders and has internalized each and every negative word about the mother-daughter relationship. The fact that fathers are hardly mentioned does not seem odd to her since we are all supposed to get along without them, but it intensifies the mother's guilt. She feels fully responsible. I often suggest that mothers stop reading this material, since it keeps them self-blaming.

Mothers experience intense feelings of failure when their daughters have trouble with food and body image. Many have been the perfect, over-functioning super-mom that their families and culture told them to be. Subconsciously, they believed this would satisfy your father and your husband and win their approval. If you have been following other people's rules, remaining loyal to the old myths about how women should be and how unimportant men are to children, rather than figuring out what is right for you and for your family, your daughter will grow up in the same way. Unsure and unaware of herself, she will try to follow tradition, be perfect, and please everyone, especially the elusive father. To help her, you need to come to terms with your own drive for perfection and your feelings of guilt and failure. Look at the origins of these emotions to determine how much they reflect your unresolved yearning for connection to your father.

Questions and New Connections

- Did you ever feel "good-enough" for your father?
- How has this affected your parenting?
- What are you teaching your daughter about guilt and perfectionism?

Seeking Help

One step toward a better balance between self and other is deciding to seek professional help for yourself, not just for your daughter. This shows that your needs and your feelings are important and that you are willing to "re-self." The problems mothers have in entering treatment surround the feelings of responsibility and failure that result from skewed roles in families—they expect that, once more, they alone will be blamed for whatever has gone wrong.

Opening the door to a therapist's office is the first step in helping you tame your guilt and stop blaming yourself. For example, through family therapy, you can develop more balance between you and your husband, or ex-husband, in the maintenance of the family's life. You also can readjust the energy you devote to others and give more to yourself after you examine how father hunger has affected the parenting roles, the division of duties, and the emotional environment in your home. Individual therapy allows a more in-depth look at the scars left from your father hunger and the ways your behavior continues to reflect it. This will help you enhance all your relationships. Parents groups, mothers groups, or family support groups can also be useful.

Questions and New Connections

- What are the biggest obstacles to your becoming involved in therapy?
- How would your father feel about your seeking help? How do your feelings about therapy reflect his?
- How can you help your daughter if you don't help yourself?

WORKING WITH HER FATHER

Now that you are aware of your own father hunger and how it may still be evident in your life as an adult, it is time to look at your current family structure and relationships. It is so easy to repeat the patterns of the past unknowingly; men and women readily adopt roles at home that do this. There are many things women can do, however, to keep children from experiencing father hunger. By separating yourself from your old ways, particularly from your tendency to take all the family responsibility, you will let your husband connect with his children. Even if you are divorced or separated, you can do this, thereby assuring that they will suffer less from father hunger than you have.

Redistributing Power and Roles

Start by assessing how you balance the see-saw of under-functioning and over-functioning between men and women in your life. It may be that your only sure power comes from over-functioning at home. Are you, like many women, gaining influence by doing everything for everyone, exhausting yourself so there's no time or energy left for you? That's not real power, that's slavery; even if you didn't see it until now, your daughter has, and her eating problems and dissatisfaction with her body are her ways of rejecting that role. You must find more real, satisfying, self-affirming authority.

To do this, you will have to stop mothering your husband, to learn to ask for help, and to determine your goals for yourself and your family. Until you alter these patterns, he doesn't have to take responsibility at home—you're treating him like another child. He can then be aloof and irresponsible, you can be angry and overwhelmed, and your children can experience father hunger firsthand.

Both of you have to change. This means that if he starts doing more in the home, you have to let him do things his way. He may not pay attention to the details that you have been socialized to think are so critical. You need to let go of that old familiar feeling that everything in the house has to be perfect—it indirectly perpetuates father hunger. Instead, allow him to find his own way of doing things. It's very difficult for women to be patient and give their husbands time to learn new jobs, but if you give sufficient time, you will work out a way to share responsibilities. This will be particularly challenging if your husband's job requires that he travel frequently. So be creative as you try to get him more involved—any participation by him is better than none. In turn, he will be more visible to the children, and your daughter will believe that men and women can support each other, work together, and share family burdens.

Questions and New Connections

- What was the power and role distribution like in your family? Is your marriage duplicating this?
- How can you begin to alter your role to let your husband into the family? What keeps you from doing this?

Escaping the Superwoman Syndrome

Many cultural patterns contribute to the difficulty women have finding balance between self and other and to the current inequality in family roles. Historically in western society, men's scripts have been singular in focus; men are to work outside the home and to provide economically. In contrast, women's roles have been more multidimensional, with many conflicting priorities to juggle: You must be a Jack(ie) of all trades. One psychologist described this as follows:

> Most women by inclination and force of circumstances will do many more things [than men do] in the course of a lifetime. The phrase 'part-time' catches a lot of the essence of the feminine style of life in a very practical sense. Women will be part-time cooks, part-time intellectuals, part-time workers. They may spend part of their life being wholly wives and mothers and another part being wholly intellectuals.[4]

This has resulted in the contemporary version of female over-functioning known as the "Superwoman Syndrome." Because of the tension many women today experience between family and career, they may pressure themselves to perform perfectly, or to over-function, in both areas. The Superwoman does it all, has it all, and needs no one. Having witnessed how her parents functioned and having experienced father hunger, she does not expect much from men. She decides that she needs no help from her husband. She is supposed to be able to do everything a man can do in addition to everything a woman can do.

In our culture, there are legitimate reasons why you might pursue this ideal. If you over-function at home and aspire to be "Superwoman," you are trying to assert power that you have not found in other ways. The only control you may feel is the private influence within the family, so if you start sharing domestic duties you relinquish some of your status. In fact, the female role is so double-binding that sometimes women don't want their husbands to be more active at home. One study found that 60% to 80% of the women did not want their husbands to do more! The research team hypothesized that these women wished to maintain the status quo of the balance of power in the family.[5] The Superwomen who are trying to do it all are struggling to attain status by doing everything at home in the traditional female world, while they succeed and work very aggressively in the traditional male world. Do you see yourself in this description?

This Superwoman Syndrome is one of the new myths that is having a severe impact on female self-esteem. Some studies have shown that the women most at risk for eating disorders are those who believe they should be totally independent, competitive, and successful in the world, denying their own need for relationships and the connectedness that is a central part of femininity.[6] They want to excel at everything and to be this new female ideal. If you can begin to revise the roles in your family so that your children see two interdependent adults sharing responsibilities, both needing the other and meeting the others' needs, you can do much to counter these destructive cultural images that contribute to the over-functioning Superwoman ideal. First, you must figure out if the Superwoman Syndrome appeals to you—and why.

Questions and New Connections

- Describe your ideal woman. Is this a Superwoman? How does your ideal fit with your parents' ideals?
- Are you satisfied with yourself as a woman?
- Is your daughter trying to be a Superwoman? Have you been pushing her to be one?

Making Room for Daddy

Daughters need their dads. Helping your daughter develop a strong connection with her father should be one of your primary goals as a mother. It requires that you separate your own needs, losses, disappointments, and anger with your father, from hers. You may have unconsciously decided that she doesn't need a father because yours was not available to you and other relationships with men have not satisfied your longing for him. Work on distinguishing your needs and desires from hers. You must survive your father hunger without sentencing her to a life with it. She is entitled to a relationship with her dad.

To "make room for daddy," you must stop protecting him from the day-to-day issues in the family. Let him know what's going on—both the good and the bad. Share the burdens of getting to appointments and lessons and doing the many other tasks you've been managing alone. Ask him to take care of some of the extended family business also, like getting birthday cards or presents. You have to be very direct and blunt and tell your husband exactly what help you need. When it comes to housework and child-care especially, you can't expect him to read your mind.

Men have never been expected to do these things before, and unlike you, your husband was not brought up to see day-to-day family life as his business. So give him some leeway. Be clear and direct about what you need from him and don't expect him to be perfect. The outcome you want is probably within reach if you define it as satisfying your children's father hunger, not as having a clean house.

As you allow your husband more active involvement in the life and responsibilities of the family, you have to control your impulses to jump into the middle of the relationships he will be establishing in the family. In earlier chapters, several women described how their mothers seemed to do too much with them because their fathers were unavailable. Although their mothers meant well, their over-involvement may have maintained the distance between the father and daughter. Moreover, their inter-ference certainly did not address the problems that kept these fathers so peripheral. Learn from their mistakes: stand by, watch, and do less interfering. You must have faith that your spouse can work out his relationship with the kids and other family members, and that, if he can't, he'll ask you for input.

You must learn to ask for help, too. In fact, when it comes to issues with the children, you probably shouldn't define your husband's role as "help." Instead, look at it as your right, your children's right, and his right. Stop seeing him as a baby sitter or a second-string quarterback who gets called into the game only if you're injured. Think of him as a peer or co-captain instead. And remember, there are basic differences between men and women that are accentuated by our socialization process. Let him find his own way of interacting with the kids. It may be different from yours but that doesn't make it wrong. If women stop supervising men and interfering with their attempts to be involved in the family, men will probably feel more comfortable and do more.

Without your efforts, the history and legacy of father hunger will be repeated in your daughter's life. Carefully look at the myths about men and see how your behaviors at home perpetuate them. Be objective and specific. For each habit of yours that keeps your spouse or ex-spouse uninvolved in the family's life and emotions, come up with an alternative behavior. This can be as simple as shopping together for a birthday present for your daughter, instead of always doing that yourself. Take inventory of all the small ways that you may be blocking the father-daughter relationship, and come up with strategies to change these. Think about how you wish your dad had been there for you and try to foster the environment and opportunities that will strengthen your daughter's connection to her dad.

Questions and New Connections

- What was your father's role in the family?
  How is your husband's similar?
- What keeps you from letting your husband into the daily life of the family?
- Would you feel insecure if he started doing more at home?

Coping with Divorce

The issues of sharing responsibility, co-parenting, and finding balance are much more difficult to manage when you are divorced. Despite your desires that your children not be hurt by your divorce, quite likely they will be, unless you work hard to understand the connections between your father hunger and the breakdown of your marriage. When a marriage ends, you lose the man who was supposed to take your father's place and satisfy all your unmet needs. Thus, you have many complicated emotions to process in order to cope with the aftermath.

To minimize your children's father hunger, you must work through your anger with your ex-spouse and resist the urge to act out through them. You also have to control your tendency to protect your children from disappointments with their father, because, in so doing, you may actually curtail his access to the children. Unresolved rage causes many divorced mothers to limit or control the relationship between the father and kids. Already burdened by the daily responsibilities for the family, more than likely you will feel resentful or jealous of the children's affection for their father. This is because, in most cases, the father does less parenting and limit-setting and offers more fun during the special time they have together.

In all these scenarios, you need to work hard to resist the impulse to misuse your power and restrict the children's time with their father or to make them choose between two parents. Because men believe all the myths about fathers' insignificance, they will too easily accept a reduced role. Then the children lose one of the most important people in their lives, and you and your ex-husband lose the possibility, no matter how remote, of sharing some of the responsibility for parenting.

Questions and New Connections

- How do your feelings about your divorce reflect residual issues between you and your dad?
- How are you influencing your daughter's relationship with her father?

HELPING YOUR DAUGHTER

In addition to working on your development of self and on your relationship with her father, there is another important way you can help your daughter deal with her father hunger. She needs to separate from you in order to connect with him, so your goal must be to let her go and let her grow.

You must communicate to your daughter that you will survive if she grows up, that being an adult woman who eats and accepts her size and shape is desirable. Show her that women can negotiate satisfying relationships with men and with a society that feels foreign and scary because of its masculine power and value system. She needs to feel that you and her father see her as a separate, important person with legitimate rights, needs, feelings, and ideas—someone who will be able to make it in the world.

Let Go—Let Grow

Young women who develop eating problems are struggling to find a personal identity—to differentiate themselves, and yet still feel attached and fulfilled in their relationships. Because female development is characterized by an ongoing connection with mother, rather than by the male experience of separation, much of the daughter's difficulties in identity formation will concern how she can be independent but still close to her mother, and how she can connect to the world of adulthood without completely losing her childhood. Your efforts here will help her be less frightened of adulthood.

Letting your daughter grow up can be a challenge. Without realizing it, you may want to keep her close and may undermine or reject her natural movement toward independence. This may sound malevolent but it's really not. You love her; in fact, you love her so much you can't let go. She fears that if she tries to be herself, she will lose you, so she chooses to give up her "self" instead. Since she already feels she lost her father, she can't risk moving away from you. So, unless you give her clear permission to grow and separate from you, and convey that you will still be there for her, she won't be able to take these steps.

Mothers show their ambivalence about a daughter's growth in various ways. Sometimes, by over-functioning, you unknowingly keep your daughter dependent on you. If you under-function, your daughter has to over-function and take care of you. She can't move away from you, because you need her too much. In these scenarios, both of you have underdeveloped selves and must strive to develop a "self." You'll have to work equally hard to find how to relate to each other to replace the old, overly close, needy way that led to these problems. Then you'll be able to let go and let grow.

Questions and New Connections

- How are you dependent on your daughter?
- How have you encouraged her to be dependent on you?
- How did your family react to your needs for more independence?

Know Her As a Person

To grow, your daughter must differentiate herself from you. But if you're too close, this will be tricky. Remember that your daughter is a separate person. See her as someone you need to get to know, instead of someone who is just like you. Try to enjoy how she's different from you, instead of feeling cut off and rejected by her individuality. Stop assuming that she feels and thinks exactly as you do. Be very clear to her about your own thoughts and feelings—use your I-voice. The more you work on your own self-development and on speaking in your I-voice, the more you will be able to help your daughter find hers.

Talk about anything with your daughter, but get her also to say how *she* feels. Encourage her to define her own thoughts, feelings, and self, separately from yours. It may be useful for her to hear how you would handle a situation she's facing, but you should avoid giving advice, or worse yet, telling her what to do. Your daughter will reject advice.

She may feel angry that you're not allowing her some independence and room to make her own decisions, but she will probably also feel guilty about not following the path you prescribe. Guilt is like quicksand for people with eating problems. There's nothing like it to get them thinking they should not eat, or should not stop eating, or should not keep the food in, or that they are not worthy of life. Try to become aware of the things you say that might provoke guilt in her. Work on this in therapy. Take responsibility for your own feelings and show interest in hers; accept that the two of you are separate and allow your connection to build in a new, adult way.

If I were to establish one rule to guide you in supporting your daughter through her recovery, it would be to try to know her as a full person, not just as "an anorexic," a "bulimic," a "dieter," or an "overeater." Mothers often worry so much about their daughters that their interactions begin to focus on the problems or symptoms rather than on the person. Consequently, women in recovery often report that friends were more helpful than family. Instead of reacting only to symptoms, friends often convey appreciation for the many dimensions of the individual. As a mother, you need to achieve a balance between confronting and acknowledging symptoms and getting past them to know the real person who is your daughter.

Questions and New Connections

- How well do your father and mother know you?
- How well do you know your daughter?
- How can you get to know her better?

Let Her Reject You

To recover from any problem, the individual has to take responsibility for it—no one else can. That doesn't mean that as a mother you should abandon your daughter and never tell her what you think. You should be talking about many things, including her eating difficulties and her relationship with her dad, and you should offer to help. But you have to offer assistance and then listen to her answer instead of offering and then immediately helping her. When she says, "No, I don't need you," accept that and let her know you still love her. Don't convey that your love is contingent on her doing things your way or even listening to you. That's another quick road to disaster.

If she rejects you, some of your own pain about being rejected by your father may surface. Get ready for feelings that you may not completely understand. You may also feel abandoned if she develops a closer relationship with her dad. These are natural events. Let them happen. Work on understanding your feelings and how they relate to your father hunger. Remember that you both need to separate from the way you have interacted in the past to make better connections in the future.

Questions and New Connections

- How do you feel when your daughter disagrees with you?
- Did you ever reject your mother? How?
- How important was this in your development?

First Steps Toward Change

To help your daughter overcome her eating and body-image conflicts, accept that you and your family environment need to change, even though you may not yet know how or why. This may be scary but it is absolutely essential, so try to get used to the idea of transformation. An important beginning is accepting that you are not totally responsible for her difficulties—her father shared in creating the family dynamics. If you believe this, you will be better able to survive the crisis and support her through recovery. Look at this as an opportunity to rebalance the self/other, separate/ connected tensions for everyone and to function more fully and more lovingly as a family. Begin by taking these steps to modify your view of her problems.

Accept that the problem is not just your daughter's eating or body-image.

Her issues with food and her body are a way of coping with her father hunger. She has been unable to connect with her dad so she has become disconnected from herself and will do anything to please others. She needs help to figure out how to relate to the masculine world and how to accept her feminine self. Until she solves these problems, she will act out her conflicts through her body.

Your job is to resist the temptation to simplify the problem, and to help her deal with the bigger issues head on. Stop looking for the old A-causes-B solutions and open yourself up to the large screen of her life and yours. Tune into your father hunger and see how it has affected both you and your daughter. Include her father in the recovery process.

Accept that she needs help from others.

Although her father probably is saying that she can "do it on her own," work with him to get professional help as soon as possible. Your daughter may need dietary counseling, medical assessment and follow-up, individual therapy, family, and possibly group therapy. Ask for direction from these professionals regarding how to handle eating at home. Let her work on her issues with food and her body individually, while you make changes within the family, support the building of a relationship between her and her dad, and encourage her development.

Be sure that you address your own reactions to her new relationships. Sometimes mothers feel replaced by their daughter's therapists or rejected if she reaches out to others. The attachment to her dad may especially bring up issues for you. Remind yourself that she needs to separate from you in order to connect with herself.

Accept that it is necessary for you to change.

Unknowingly, you have brought your father hunger to your marriage and your parenting. Your daughter needs you to change so she can have a different kind of relationship with you, with her dad, with herself, with food, and with the world—relationships that are free of father hunger. If she sees you addressing emotional issues, she'll feel safer as she figures out what she should do to improve her life. She will be less scared that you will reject her if she alters her relationship with you and becomes more connected to her dad.

As you address your own disappointment in your relationship with your father, in your marriage, and in your life, you will model for her that change is desirous and beneficial. She will believe that if you can overcome problems, she will be able to as well.

Accept that you may have some unhealthy attitudes toward food or weight.

Your attitudes, self-esteem, and body-image all reflect your reactions to your own father hunger. If you have tried to please your father or other men through your appearance, by losing weight, eating less, or pursuing the "perfect" body, you will have to work hard to change your own beliefs and practices to help her.

The children most at risk for developing eating problems come from families that stress appearance and convey that weight is volitional and an example of self-control and personal achievement. Young women growing up with mothers who show preoccupation with their weight and dieting and who derive their self-esteem through their appearance, are expecially at risk for eating disorders.[7] If you have criticized your daughter's body, or encouraged her dieting, or even competed with her about weight loss or management, you have contributed to her problems.

To support you daughter's recovery, you will have to face these issues yourself. You need to be honest about the meaning and importance you give to weight and body-image and how these reflect your desire to please men. Like your daughter, you have grown up in a culture that is not friendly or accepting of the range of female body sizes. You must figure out how you have responded to that to help your daughter find peace with her physical needs.

Accept that her father may need to be more involved in her life.

By now you probably realize that you can't make everything all better. Hopefully, you also see that you did not cause all her problems. The next step is to encourage a better connection between her and her father. You may need to work through your own feelings about him, and admit if you feel jealous of their relationship. The goal must be to foster love, openness, and personal development—to let your daughter go and grow.

CHAPTER 12

◆ ◆ ◆

HOW DAUGHTERS CAN COPE WITH FATHER HUNGER

For too many young women, father hunger knocks the balance between self and other out of whack. Craving a relationship with this special man, they will do anything to please him, other men, or authority figures to win male approval. Although the intention is to connect with dad, the result is a separation from self and a general sense of disconnection from life.

To heal, you must begin a process of self-discovery and resolution of your father hunger so that you can forge a path in the world as a strong, assertive young woman, able to withstand the constant messages you receive about weight, beauty, dieting, slimness, fashion, and appearance, and to manage your doubts about how to please men. This chapter examines how you can readjust this balance between self and other—first by focusing on your self, next by connecting to your dad, and then by concentrating on your family, social relationships, and culture.

CONNECTING WITH YOURSELF

You have to get back to the basics. Learning "the three Rs" in school was probably easy for you. Now it's time to learn a new set of three Rs: Recovery Requires Reconnection. To heal your father hunger and get your life back on track you must first reconnect with yourself. The only way to do this is by slowly separating from your eating disorder. You can start this process by learning about the function of your symptoms, discovering the pain they have covered up and the things they are trying to accomplish. Gradually you will understand their true meaning—how they expressed the hunger for father and for other connections that you couldn't put into words. Then you can begin to face the facts of your eating disorder by admitting, confronting, and changing your behaviors around food and your body. In this way, separating from your eating disorder will allow you to reconnect with yourself.

Your attitudes and behaviors around food are very important to you or else you would not continue them. In some complex, maybe unconscious, way, you started them hoping they would help you deal with life. This initial intention, however, has become confused and you may no longer have any idea if they are working for you or against you.

When I ask patients why they have developed an eating problem serious enough for them to enter a special hospital program, they usually say, "I just stopped eating," or "I just wanted to lose weight," or other simple, "I just...." statements. Like each of my patients, you'll have to find out for yourself how your eating problems have helped you cope with your life. But you must start by accepting that they're not "just" anything. Instead, they are complicated cover-ups of other conflicts. One woman who has struggled with eating problems for many years recently said to me, "'just' is a four-letter word." She knows she has to dig deeper into her inner self whenever she hears herself say, "I just...." She's right. It takes a long time to figure out the function of your symptoms and how they relate to your father hunger.

As you begin the process of connecting with yourself and understanding how you ended up with these problems, you may still be searching for one experience or one person to blame. Human behavior doesn't fit into a simple cause/effect model, so allow yourself to see the bigger picture of feelings, relationships, and interconnections. Resist the "I only wanted...." or "It's just that ...." simplifications—they're misleading. No one is to blame for your problems with food—not your father, not your mother, not your family, not your friends. Your symptoms were the only way you could express your pain. Although your family has been hurt by your problems, this was not your intention. You are not to blame either. Start this section by trying to forgive yourself and your family—no one is to blame.

Once you acknowledge that your symptoms are more than "just" anything, think about how they functioned for the women we have discussed in earlier chapters. Many had hoped to gain power or control over their lives by limiting their appetites; others sought this through overeating or hurting their bodies by purging or excessive exercise. For some it was a way to achieve, please others, and prove their self-worth.

Quite simply, your symptoms have separated you from yourself, despite your initial intention that they would connect you to your dad and other people. Look carefully at what you avoid through your problems with food. You must face these disappointments, losses, conflicts, and feelings to reconnect with yourself.

Discovering the Hidden Meaning

Your symptoms have meaning. They represent your inner wishes and feelings, but at the same time they insidiously separate you from them. Overtly, they communicate to others that you want to be left alone, that you need no one, that you will get through life with your eating disorder as your best friend. Underneath, however, you desperately want a connection, especially to your dad. Take the time to discern what your eating problems say to others and what they really mean to you. You may find a huge gap between the two. Here are some examples:

Not Loving Yourself—Feeling Unloved by Dad

One statement that your eating problems make to other people is that you don't value yourself. The true meaning of your behavior, though, is that you have not felt loved by others, especially by your dad. You can't fully love and accept yourself because you haven't been given these feelings by the key people in your life. You must gradually explore what your experiences of love have been within your family and within the relationship to your father. To get better, you must face this head-on instead of eating, starving, overexercising, or purging the feelings away.

Being Successful in the Male World—Feeling Unappreciated by Dad

Your behaviors around food and your body express an acceptance of many masculine values and behaviors. Self-control, excessive exercise, denial of feelings and needs, and lean, hard bodies are signs of achievement for men, and you have pursued these heartily. Yet they really represent a deep feeling that your dad does not appreciate or value you. You need him to acknowledge you as a female, but the only way you have found to do this is through being more male. You must reconnect to your femininity and become aware of how the things you have done to please men have effectively separated you from important parts of yourself as a woman.

Behaving Rigidly—Covering Up Inner Turmoil

Others who look at you see someone who appears driven and self-confident. What they don't know is that inside you are horribly confused about your feelings, decisions, beliefs, values, relationships, and future. The rigidity of your eating problems covers up this insecurity. It provides safety and predictability and keeps you from the chaos of your world. Once more, however, the real meaning of your behavior is an unmet desire for connection. Your symptoms mask your confusion about how to be a person and how to be accepted by your dad and others. The only way to create a real, self-based identity is to separate from these old ways of avoidance, admit how cut-off you are from yourself, and begin to build a life free from your symptoms.

Maintaining Distance—Wanting Closeness

The conflicts surrounding body-image and food that accompany eating problems instantly and pervasively create distance between self and other. People often conclude that you don't want a relationship with them when you refuse invitations due to your fear of eating in public or being seen as fat. Gradually you exclude yourself from social activities, family events, and from relationships, but this all started because people were so important to you! In fact, you want to please them and be liked, but many of your actions tell them to leave you alone. Again, although the desire is for closeness, your symptoms are separating you. Your dad, like most people in your life, doesn't know the hidden meaning of your behavior, and, with all his masculine baggage about separation, will easily let you alone. You must learn more about how you subconsciously convert your desire for closeness into behavior that creates distance.

Denying All Feelings—Being Overwhelmed by Your Emotions

Others look at you and see a well-defended fortress—someone who admits to no feelings, maybe even someone who "can deal with anything." Your inner reality is different from this. You, in fact, have very few ways to cope, and thus, rely on your eating disordered behaviors to avoid anger and pain. Your feelings about your dad are among the most difficult. The only way you are sure to maintain equilibrium is by denying your discomfort with him and with everything else. The result is an agonizing separation

The only solution is to slowly confront your inner life. In fact, you have powerful, frightening feelings and an emptiness that gnaws at you. Satisfying your hunger for connection, especially with your father, will begin to fill the void and will provide support as you learn how to cope more directly with feelings.

Questions and New Connections

- How do your eating and body image problems keep you from knowing yourself?
- What feelings about your father have you been trying to avoid? What will happen if you express these directly?
- What did your dad teach you about feelings?
- How do your eating problems reflect his messages about emotional expression?

Getting Support

The most difficult fact you must face is that in order to connect with yourself and with relationships, you must separate from your eating disorder. When actively symptomatic, you focus on food, calories, your body, and weight. These become obsessions—nothing else seems important. Your symptoms keep you from

recognizing feelings and numb you from the pain in your relationships. You must acknowledge that you have used food to avoid
other issues. Confront your problems head-on and normalize your
eating! This will take hard work but it pays off. You will begin to
replace your conflicted conceptions about food and your negative
obsession about your body with more positive experiences and
find ways to have real and satisfying interactions with other
people—even with your dad. For the first time, you will learn how
to balance your self/other, separate/connected tensions.

To initiate the process of reconnection, start by admitting that
you could use some help. Entering treatment is a good first step
toward this goal because it challenges all those old notions of
yours. Therapy is for everyone else, but not for you, right? You say
you don't need it, but you have a problem that could kill you.
You're sad, lonely, overwhelmed. Friends and family don't seem
to know how to help. You feel terrified and out of control, but
entering therapy means you can't take care of everything yourself.
It means giving up the masculine act of not needing anyone, and
it frightens you.

As in other addictive behaviors, you may have to "hit bottom"
before you can admit to needing any help. Each person will
experience this in a different way. For Karen, "hitting bottom"
occurred when she could no longer deny her physical symptoms.

> I realized I had a problem when I wanted to eat but couldn't, and
> started falling apart in school. Friends had tried, doctors had tried, but
> I was the one who had to convince myself. The day I couldn't walk I
> was scared—I woke up and couldn't feel my legs. The doctors couldn't
> find anything wrong with them. I finally realized I was hurting me. The
> two hospitalizations hadn't convinced me, but this did. Then I started
> eating and talking to my therapist.

For others, "hitting bottom" is a more spiritual or abstract
experience. Suzanne reported this encounter with herself:

> It was something I had to do for myself.... I remember the turning point—it was almost mystical. I couldn't sleep at night and would be awake very early. One morning I got up for a walk around 6 o'clock. It was going to be a beautiful summer day. I felt the sun, leaned against a tree and realized that I had felt good for a second. I hadn't felt happy in so long—it felt so good. I decided I deserved it, that it wasn't worth it to keep going the way I was. I remember walking in the house and making a peanut butter and jelly sandwich. I still thank God for sunny days. I needed therapy but I hadn't been ready until then.

Even after hitting bottom, you may be distrustful of therapy. You may be imitating your dad or trying to be Superwoman—in either case, you're not supposed to need anyone. In relationships, you've been the giver; it's hard to think about one where you might receive or where the self/other balance would be different. You probably worry about what your therapist is going to expect and whether you're going to be able to measure up, since you desperately want approval and haven't gotten it from your dad. You can't imagine a relationship that's for you. Yours have felt like constant demands and disappointments, so you may be skeptical about the benefits of treatment.

If your approach to recovery duplicates the masculine model— insisting that you need no one, trying to do everything yourself, controlling life by thinking away your problems, never admitting you're sad—it's probably not going to work. Even if you can manage to change your eating and treat your body better, this may not be enough. You need to understand why your conflicts with food and your body developed and to see your problems and emotions not as demons or enemies but as tools for change. Your feelings need to be aired, not buried, and therapy is the best place for this to start.

In therapy, you have to stop wearing a mask. The expectation is that you be yourself. You may not know who are under this anorexic mask, bulimic mask, or perfect-little-girl mask, and a therapist can help you along this scary road of self-discovery.

Therapists are guides, trained to help others identify, understand, and express their feelings. In this safe arena, you can examine your disappointments with your dad and how your father hunger still affects you. Working with a therapist will show you how to express yourself and get your needs met, how to balance self and other, and how to be separate and connected in more satisfying ways in all relationships.

A therapist who has training and experience in eating disorders can be especially useful. A specialist will know when you need more additional professional support and who the local experts are for the medical complications that accompany eating problems. This is especially important if you have been symptomatic for a long time. Regardless of the length of time, however, anyone with these unhealthy behaviors is at risk for serious medical complications, especially those related to cardiac functioning, hormone production, fertility, bone formation, and digestive problems. Because each of us is unique biochemically, people can have medical complications at any point. Discuss this early in your treatment.

A specialist can also help you make sense of the feelings about your body associated with the changes in your eating patterns. He or she can help you to see how these experiences fit into the long-term recovery process. Although you may feel hopeless, weird, or stuck, an experienced therapist may see positive signs of recovery.

Specialists can also identify interaction patterns in your family that should be addressed, and will work with you to understand your family-of-origin, your place within it, and the unhealthy interactions you're duplicating in other relationships. A therapist can help you distinguish the people from the pattern in your family, so you will feel less guilty exploring family issues. You will surely feel sad as you give up your illusions about your childhood and recognize the pain and problems that existed there. Therapy will support you through this as well.

The best description I can give about the experience of therapy comes from a patient of mine who compared recovery to climbing a mountain. To her I was someone to lean back on when she felt lonely, scared, helpless, or tired. She knew I would hold her up and she wouldn't fall backward. Gradually she has found ways to support herself and no longer needs me as much.

Formal therapy is not the only road to recovery, although it may be the safest one for most people. In addition, you can find help by participating in support groups, attending lectures, reading books, doing new things, exploring religious or other spiritual beliefs, and just by talking to people. The important things is to open up to a new approach and to depart from what is compromising your life.

Facing the facts includes admitting that you probably don't even know what you like and don't like, what is "real" or how to be a "real" person because you have been so absorbed by your problems with food and your body. The best description of being "real" I have found is in *The Velveteen Rabbit* .[1] No matter how old you are, I recommend that you read this children's story. A child's toys express great wisdom in this book. Here's my favorite excerpt:

> "What is real?" asked the Rabbit one day. "Does it mean having things that buzz inside you and a stick-out handle?"
> "Real isn't how you are made," said the Skin Horse. "It's a thing that happens to you. When a child loves you for a long, long time, not just to play with, but REALLY loves you, then you become Real. It doesn't happen all at once. You become. It takes a long time. Generally by the time you are Real, most of your hair has been loved off, and your eyes drop out and you get loose in the joints and very shabby. But these things don't matter at all, because once you are Real you can't be ugly, except to people who don't understand."

Recovery is becoming "real" just as the Skin Horse defines it. If you are real, you value relationships and love over your appearance or weight. You no longer constantly try to "look good" or be "perfect." You accept yourself for who you are and you accept others for who they are. You no longer wear a mask that is intended to please others; you act from your heart; you're honest and open and allow others to truly know you.

To be real and to love your own self, you have to stop being perfect. You can't be daddy's little girl any more. Even if his love is unconditional, you will never know it because you'll believe he loves the "perfect" little girl—not the real you. Just as you have to let go of the Superman myth for your father, let go of your self-imposed Superwoman or perfect-little-girl image. The resulting reconnection with yourself will gradually lead to recovery.

Questions and New Connections

- Have you ever been real, just yourself, with anyone?
- What masks do you wear to keep yourself from being real with your dad? What if you stopped wearing these?
- Can your father accept you for who you really are?
- What frightens you about getting better and being real?

CONNECTING TO YOUR FATHER

Despite what you have experienced growing up in our culture, you have the right to two parents. And fathers have the right to be involved in their family's emotional lives. Try conceptualizing a revised script for your future relationship with your father and with men in general. Use what you have learned from the "bad times" with food to help you improve your relationship with your dad and to put more "good times" into your life-script. At best, you and your father can meet for the first time as two open, caring people. At least, you can discontinue the cycle and consequences of father hunger in your life.

The time you devote to this will be well invested because the relationship with your dad is a blueprint for all interactions with men. Remember, history will repeat itself unless you work hard to change the painful family patterns and father hunger in your life. The anxiety you felt about whether you were doing enough for him has diminished your self-esteem, your self-confidence, your identity, and your acceptance of your body and sexuality. It is important to understand your connection with your dad, even if you can't change it. He may live too far away, be ill, or dead, or his own problems may make him incapable of having a relationship. But if you work on understanding your bond with him, you can prevent the anxiety, disappointments, losses, and expectations you have experienced, from compromising your connections with boyfriends, spouses, friends, bosses, and men in general. Not only do you have the right to two parents, you also have rights in relationships with men. You will be better able to assert them if you have worked on your connection to your dad.

Give Your Dad a Chance

Just as each of you is unique and has developed similar symptoms for very different reasons, your father also deserves individual understanding. He merits more than collective accusations that he has not been perfect—he was probably doing the best he could within the constraints of a very limited social role and an impossible mythic image. He doesn't know how to connect with you. Give the two of you a chance. Forgive him for his imperfections and awkwardness.

Even if your dad is not available, you still have the right to know about him. Try talking to relatives or family friends to get the information he can't give you directly. Remind yourself that just as many things contributed to your eating disorder, so a combination of circumstances also affected your father's personality and functioning as a parent. Learn whatever you can about these things. For example, if one of his parents was an alcoholic, you can read literature from Alcoholics Anonymous or Adult Children of Alcoholics to help you understand what his life may have been like. If he grew up during a time of social change or political unrest, read about these events. Non-fiction will give you facts but fiction may give you more of a feeling as to how the events affected him personally. In fact, instead of reading one more book about eating disorders, consider reading a book that will help you understand your father. If you understand his life, you may more easily forgive him for his limitations as a father.

Once you understand the cultural myths men experience and know more about your dad as an individual, you can develop more realistic expectations for your relationship. You also may be able to help him change and work with him through some of the existing barriers to his role in the family. For example, now, when we ask fathers to be more emotionally open and involved at home, we're "double-binding" them by placing two mutually exclusive demands on them. That is, we expect fathers to take care of us, to protect us, and to be brave, strong, powerful, and invulnerable in the world, but we also want them to be emotionally aware, to disclose their feelings, and to be vulnerable and intimate. It's especially unfair because we have changed our requirements so suddenly and offer little help to make these changes.

Use Your I-Voice

You can improve both your self-development and your relationship with your dad by working through your own double-bind of having feelings but not expressing them. In the last chapter I spoke about the need for mothers to develop an "I-voice," but you need to do this too.

Your blaming voice says, "You were never there for me, dad." He may have wanted to be there but he was fulfilling the myths and expectations society had for him. If you speak in your blaming voice, it's likely he will feel misunderstood and stop listening. He may cover up his feelings of inadequacy by expressing anger, and will probably feel baffled or helpless about how to connect with you.

To prevent these misunderstandings, be specific and use your I-voice: "I felt you didn't really care about me because you spent so much time at work." Your dad is human too; contrary to the old myths, he has feelings. So, like the rest of us, he'll respond better to love and support than he will to accusations. As you speak in your I-voice about your experience as a daughter, you can be a model of communication for your dad. You may be ahead of him in this area, but be patient and give him a chance to learn.

Communicating and connecting with your dad doesn't mean, however, that you have to always agree. In fact, you should be disagreeing! If your parents aren't complaining about the "generation gap," you probably haven't developed enough of your "self" yet. Maybe you're protecting them from what's new and different when you should be challenging them to understand how the world has changed since they were your age.

Let Go of the Old and Connect With the New

As you learn about the real person your father is and forgive him for his imperfections, you will be able to let go of that mythic father who was magically supposed to meet all your needs and protect you from all problems. If you discard this image, you will probably feel a loss of something very important—maybe the security blanket of childhood or being "daddy's little girl." However, you might gain an honest relationship with your father, something far more satisfying than an empty and outdated myth.

You may be frightened of taking these steps. For some of you, this fear is based on the reality of an explosive or abusive father.

If this is your situation, you have to carefully decide how, when, and whether to be more emotionally involved with your father. Look to your therapist for guidance as you make these decisions. For many others, however, the fear of getting to know your father is based on the myths about men's lack of emotions and apathy about parenting. If you talk with your dad, these beliefs may come tumbling down.

Some of you may be able to address your father hunger and work on these steps with the support and involvement of your dad. Others may face fathers who have neither the interest nor the ability to understand their past relationships and improve their future. Although it's worth the effort to approach your dad on these issues, you may have to accept that he cannot deal with your father hunger, nor with his own. Keep working on your recovery anyway. You may be fortunate and find other men in your life who can be emotionally available, nurturant, and loving. They will never replace your father but you may still be able to enjoy a close relationship with a man. Think about uncles, grandfathers, family friends, teachers, or clergymen as potential resources as you confront your feelings about your father. A male therapist might be useful as well. His understanding will validate your feelings. Be sure to process your father hunger as much as possible so that it doesn't continue to color every interaction you have with men.

Questions and New Connections

- How much do you know about your dad's life? How could you find out more?
- Does this explain why you have had problems being close to each other? To other men?
- What can you change in your current relationship with your father?

CONNECTING TO YOUR FAMILY

Establishing a new relationship with your father or reconciling yourself to the old one is not the end of your work. That relationship does not exist in a vacuum; instead, it is part of a larger family and social context. Your father's role and behavior have affected all of your interactions. Any work you do to connect with your self or with your father makes ripples throughout the whole system. Everyone has suffered and needs healing in some way, although other family members may be unwilling or unable to recognize this.

Even though your family may refuse to face the fact that your eating problems reflect underlying family issues, you need to face this. As one woman described it:

> To recover I had to recognize all the pain in my life. But I also had to accept that I could only change me, not my family. They were not interested in therapy or in talking about our problems. I had felt so deprived, but I just had to accept that and learn how to fill my own needs. Once I did, I was able to eat a cookie without eating the whole box and I didn't have to starve myself any more.

Once you have uncovered your pain, eased your guilt, said good-bye to your idyllic view of a "perfect" family, your protective armor is gone. Give yourself time to accept this loss. It will be especially difficult if your family is unable to support you. You might feel stuck in anger, sadness, misunderstanding, and disappointments for a while, but with the help of therapy you should be able to move on with your life. Liz was caught for a long time in her rage with her parents and her dream that they would change. Gradually, her therapist helped her to separate from the pain and fantasies of her childhood and connect with her future. This is how she described the effect of one of her individual therapy sessions:

My doctor said, "Your parents win either way. If you die, they get lots of sympathy. If you gain weight, they'll be able to brag about their daughter who got through all this and recovered from this disease." I realized he was right. I was wasting my life because of all the horror in my family and only I could change that.

Like Liz, you must accept that your needs and disappointments are real. Stop wasting time fantasizing about how things could have been different. Acknowledging your losses and your pain is a step toward healing.

Revise Your Relationships

Now that you recognize how much your father's distance and unavailability have affected you, consider how this colored your relationship with your mother. Growing up, you probably had no idea what her life was really like as she carried the burdens of the family's dad-to-day routine. Take another look at your childhood and your family's life. Talk to your mother about how disappointments with your father contributed to a shared unhappiness and how family scripts got in the way of your relationship with her. Discuss the trouble you've had balancing self with other. If she isn't available or willing to talk in this way, it's still worthwhile for you to figure out how your disconnection with your father has affected your connection with her.

Now translate how your father's script affected your connections with your siblings. Quite likely you have wounds to heal in your relationships with them. You may have competed for his attention and affection and never felt comfortable with each other, or you may feel slighted and misunderstood because your siblings don't understand your problems or won't discuss the family's emotional patterns. Again, it is worth your time to try to process these with them. With or without their self-disclosure, try to understand what was happening as you all grew up; the more pieces of the puzzle you find, the more you'll comprehend why your eating problems emerged.

Part of becoming a whole person is developing your own separate relationships with members of the extended family. While growing up, children usually relate to other relatives through their parents (often their mothers), but this limits the interactions. These relatives know you based on your family's script for you and you are similarly acquainted with them. If you meet them on a more individual basis, you will learn a lot about your family, for you'll see things from another perspective. In turn, you will discover new things about yourself, and more of the pieces to your life's puzzle will be apparent. Who knows, you may find support and caring in these relationships to help you weather the challenges you face in recovery.

Find a New Role

Separating from your old ways of interacting, finding balance between your needs and other's, and expressing your feelings directly instead of through your body and eating, necessitates a new role for you in your family. You'll have to assert yourself, instead of caving into every demand or subtle hint at home. You must become more grounded in yourself and more aware of why you do what you do in these relationships. Others may be unwilling to change, but you can still alter your script in the family; they will have to adjust. Gradually the system will change and there will be more room for you and your needs. However, the burden is on you to educate the family about who you really are and what you want from them.

In your family, quite likely you have been pegged as the "sick one," the "anorexic," the "bulimic," the "black sheep," or labeled in some other limited way. It's hard work to extract yourself from such an image, because families get stuck with labels and scripts and often resist change. Your symptoms have created a barrier, which you must dismantle.

If other members are willing to participate, family therapy can be useful to this process of reconnection. There you can work on asserting yourself more in a safe and supportive atmosphere. The whole family can learn how to show love and caring and to communicate more directly with each other.

Questions and New Connections

- How did your father's role at home influence your relationship with your mother? Your siblings?

- Which family members could support you as you address your father hunger and your recovery? What keeps you from asking them for help?

- Can you remember a time when you asserted yourself with your family on an issue other than your eating or your body? What did it feel like?

CONNECTING TO YOUR WORLD

The transformation you have been experiencing in your relationship to yourself, your father, and your family will not stop there. Once you separate from your old method of avoiding feelings through your eating problems and you reconnect to yourself, anything is possible. Resolving your father hunger and issues with your family are the first steps toward translating your internal changes into external behaviors.

Gradually all your relationships will reflect your new-found self-esteem. Other people—parents, siblings, relatives, friends, lovers, acquaintances, peers, co-workers, bosses, teachers—will see a strong, connected person negotiating interactions and giving both self and others compassion and validation. What you are discovering is personal power. You can balance your needs with those of others. You no longer need to starve, overeat, or exercise away your father hunger and self-doubt.

This sense of inner-strength will also be evident in your relationship to the culture at large. You will tolerate and withstand the negative forces that overwhelm women and exclude men in families; forces that invalidate females by reducing their worth to weight, appearance, and restraint of their eating and other appetites. You may even begin to challenge these cultural mores. You will encourage others to defy these limitations and standards and to be themselves. You will use your connection to yourself to help others to separate from their unhealthy ways of coping with the father hunger these forces represent.

Through your recovery, you will inadvertently and unconsciously help others. Because you are different, the world is also going to be different. The "three R's"—Recovery Requires Reconnection—may even expand to Reconnection Results in Revolution as your new way of being in relationships empowers others to also reconnect with themselves, resolve their father hunger, and find a place in the world. The individual changes you make can eventually lead to a transformed society where men and women complement and understand each other and girls grow up feeling valued, accepted, and loved by both parents. Father hunger will gradually fade, and women, now able to balance self and other, will no longer endanger their health to win approval from men. What a revolution!

Questions and New Connections

- How might resolving your father hunger change your life? What would be different for you?
- What is your place in the world?

CHAPTER 13

◆ ◆ ◆

WHY WE ALL MUST
PREVENT FATHER HUNGER

We have covered much territory as we have explored father hunger—its origins, its manifestations, and its solutions. I hope this has enabled you to see that men do not necessarily choose to be uninvolved, nor are they physiologically or psychologically destined to be remote fathers. The role we have given them, however, too often results in men feeling unappreciated and left out of the family. Yet, if given the opportunity, men can be positively and wonderfully involved with their children. We know that fathers can do it, but now we have to create a system that will allow it to occur more frequently.

These changes in men's roles and family life are not really an option or a choice: they are a necessity! Life is becoming more and more complex for each generation. There are many threats to children's physical and psychological well-being, especially our negative attitudes toward the female body, our obsession with weight and dieting, our constant exposure to perfection, and the technological, nature-defying products and practices incessantly marketed to promote these fixations. You have seen that the power of these threats is greater when a girl has not felt loved and accepted by her dad as she struggles with her changing body during adolescence.

Father hunger contributes to many other mental health and behavior problems in children and adolescents. We find clear links between the nature of the father-child relationship and child and adolescent psychopathology in areas such as juvenile delinquency, conduct disorder, school failure, and impulsive behaviors.[1] Teachers, counselors, school administrators, and therapists often find themselves concluding that children's problems might be reduced if their fathers were more actively involved in their lives. So, for the sake of all children—the girls who will internalize their hurt, disappointment, and rejection and will endanger their health by battling their bodies, and the boys who will externalize their anger and act out in a manner that is both self-destructive and destructive to others—we must end father hunger.

In the Appendices, I have targeted a few professions that have tremendous influence on children and families. I have conceptualized how people in these roles could help to reverse father hunger. For each of the groups, I have also suggested strategies to stimulate your thinking about what you can do to begin the change process. We must make men a more integral part of the family, give women more security and respect in their role in the world, and help children to grow up with the resources they need to survive in a culture that promotes unhealthy eating, emphasizes appearance and weight, and pits masculinity and femininity against each other. Use these ideas as a springboard for your own. They are only a beginning, but they may point you in the right direction.

I hope that you will take the information, ideas, and suggestions from this book to effect change in your own relationships and to work toward the systematic changes that will improve all of our lives. Often, when we think about major social issues such as father hunger, we conclude that the problems are beyond our control. They seem huge and insurmountable, and we feel help-less and powerless by comparison. However, there is always something we can do. We can change ourselves, for each of us impacts many other people. Begin by getting rid of those old myths about men and about how their daughters don't need them. Recognize how you have needed your father and how he was or was not able to meet your needs.

After you face your own scars or wounds from your relation-ship with your dad, you'll be able to help the men in your life have fuller, more emotionally-connected lives. Think of how to create new scripts that will empower both men and women to achieve their potential as individuals, partners, or parents. If you person-ally try to pave a more positive role for fathers so that men and women can begin to share power and responsibility in the family, you will help to reverse father hunger. Remember: if you're not part of the solution, you're part of the problem.[2]

It is time to rewrite the old myths and scripts. Each of you must figure out how to combine the pain of the past with your hopes for the future and how to separate from the old ways of being together and connect to the new. With your hard work, commitment, and creativity, life will be better for everyone. Imagine a world where both men and women feel comfortable, powerful, supported, valued, and loved. Imagine what would happen if we could raise children in an environment with men and women equally sharing responsibility and caretaking. Imagine adolescent females feeling welcomed into the adult world and no longer having to prove their worth through their appearance or weight. Imagine fathers feeling satisfied, included, and connected. Imagine both men and women finding balance between self and other, between separateness and connectedness. Imagine a way to be part of the solution and no longer part of the problem.

APPENDIX A

◆ ◆ ◆

SUGGESTED STRATEGIES FOR EDUCATORS

The educational system is an invaluable resource for designing family or cultural change because most families with children are involved in some private or public school setting. In fact, more and more children are enrolled in formal day care from infancy onward, making it possible to prevent problems, or at least to recognize them early.

If you question whether schools should be involved in family problems or cultural change, consider the roots of the word "educate." Its Latin origins suggest leadership, for "educare" means "to lead out of." The educational system can help to lead us out of the current state of men's impaired parenting by providing some solutions to father hunger. Already, many male educational staff play an important ancillary role in children's lives. Often male teachers, coaches, guidance counselors, or principals find themselves spending extra time with boys who show the need for paternal attention. Unfortunately, because of our myths about girls development, many caring male educators have not realized how they can help female students.

Schools are already faced with the results of our current dysfunctional family systems. Involving them in prevention makes sense.

Build a Constructive Role for Men in Families

*   **Educators** should get to know the fathers of their students. Schedule meetings or phone conversations before work or in the evening, since men may feel unable to leave their jobs during the day. Be sure to share information equally with both parents; avoid using mother as the only link to the family.

*   **Schools** can get fathers involved more directly by finding out if they have any special skills, knowledge, or hobbies that could be utilized in educational programs. Community-based programs can do the same.

*   **Schools** can also use their male staff members as models to show how men can provide emotional support, nurturance, and interest to children.

*   Both **schools** and **community groups** can sponsor discussions on parenting that focus on fathering or ways parents can work together effectively even when they are stressed by divorce, dual careers, and other problems. It can be particularly useful to educate parents about how much the world, the educational system, and the social environment have changed since they grew up.

Encourage Healthy Attitudes about Food, Weight, and Body-image

*   **Day-care centers, pre-schools,** and **schools** should sponsor programs to teach parents about nutrition and about managing children's eccentric tastes or food refusal. Your State Department of Health or Department of Education can usually provide personnel, ideas, or materials for such programs.

- **Child-care centers** and **schools** should make meals and snack-times pleasant, calm periods and should avoid utilizing food as a reward or punishment for other behaviors. By paying attention to the quality of food and the structure of mealtime, they can be certain that children have appetizing and nutritious food, enough time to eat, and an environment conducive to digestion and enjoyment of food.

- **Science, home economics,** and **health educators** should incorporate nutrition into their curricula and should teach not just what we should eat but why we should eat it. Let students know that nutritional needs and drives change as we grow and that our appetites often intensify when our bodies are changing or growing. Be sure to teach both sexes about nutrition; too often, we assume that food is the female's exclusive domain.

- **Coaches** and **physical educators** should include nutrition in their discussions with athletes, and be cautious about advising students to lose weight. If they believe that weight loss is absolutely necessary, they should provide guidance about how to do this safely and should be sure that the youngster does not lose too much.

- **Coaches** and **physical educators** should both model and endorse a healthy lifestyle, with stable nutrition and exercise habits. If a student athlete engages in self-destructive behaviors to change body weight, such as excessive dieting, vomiting, fasting, or abusing laxatives, diuretics, or other medications, this should be addressed.

- **Educators** in all content areas and grades can influence children's emerging body-image. See suggestions for "Pediatricians and other family-care physicians" in Appendix B.

- All **schools** should end the recent practice of measuring and posting students' body-fat compositions. In most cases, these measurements are done inaccurately. This conveys misinformation to children and may contribute to body-image dissatisfaction and destructive eating habits.

Address Self-Esteem, Communication Skills, and Problem-Solving

- **Day-care personnel** and **educators** should ask parents to count how many compliments and how many criticisms they give to their children each day. Suggest a minimum ratio of five compliments to each criticism. If parents reveal that their left-over issues from childhood are getting in the way, suggest some reading or even some counseling to reverse these patterns. Help fathers, especially, to understand the effects even their off-handed remarks have on their children.

- **Educational approaches** and **other child-oriented activities** should emphasize communication and give children opportunities to say what they think. Building communication does not just happen in English classes. Encourage art, music, and other modalities for self-expression. Convey appreciation for the child's efforts no matter what the finished product is like.

- **Schools** should also teach children about decision-making. Help them figure out how to get the information that will allow them to make choices. Encourage them to differentiate between opinions and facts and between emotion and logic and to find ways to balance both sides when making a decision. Ask them to describe a problem they face and how they should solve it. Convey that no decision is perfect—they just have to find what fits them best! Special projects in areas such as drama or health education can provide opportunities to make various responses to difficult situations. Through role play, encourage youngsters to find alternative ways to solve problems and to cope with parents, peer pressure, and anxiety about achievement.

Provide Resources on Eating Disorders

• Throughout many different programs and messages to students and their families, **schools** should try to demystify therapy and mental health problems. Convey that we all need help from time to time, so it will be easier for a family to accept this when it finds itself in need. Let fathers know how important their support is both in preventing problems and in overcoming them.

• **Schools** and **other systems** involved with children, adolescents, and young adults should train all staff members to recognize the warning signs and symptoms of eating disorders. They should also advise staff of the process to follow should they be concerned about a youngster. Having a team in place within the school to assess the problem and plan the intervention is essential. The **school team** should decide who can best approach the student and family. Usually it is advantageous to share concerns with the student directly and then contact the family. Remember to include the father in your discussions. The professionals should be direct and honest about what information they have and be sensitive to the student and parents. Help the parents to take charge and make decisions.

• **Schools** should know the area resources for treating eating disorders and give this information to the parents. Advise that the youngster be seen as soon as possible by the primary physician to assess his or her medical status. Ask for permission to call the doctor and share the school's observations. Also, let the family know that you will be monitoring the situation and calling them to be sure they have sought help.

- In all your communications to the student and family, be supportive. They all will have difficulty facing the problem and will suffer from guilt and self-doubt. Try not to be judgmental or blaming; remember how complicated the causes of eating problems are and that no one wanted this to happen. Aim at developing a working alliance between the school and family.

- If the family refuses help and the situation appears severe (for instance, the student faints or falls at school), treat it as you would any other life-threatening situation. Bring your team together and consider referring the case to your State Department of Protective Services if the student is under 18. If over 18, you may need legal and medical advice to help you plan other approaches. It is worthwhile to continue to try to get the student and family to agree to treatment.

◆ ◆ ◆

SUGGESTED STRATEGIES FOR PHYSICIANS

A doctor's words or prescriptions are usually valued highly by families. Thus, physicians should consider how they can use their position of trust and authority to facilitate the changes in family structure that will expand men's roles and promote children's emotional well-being and security. A child's health and development is not just a physical process, so pediatricians should also attend to psychological issues. Male physicians can model a nurturant, supportive interaction with children and can discuss with fathers how to be more comfortable and involved in their children's emotional and physical care. Both male and female physicians should pay attention to the messages they give about parental roles and duties and should try to equalize the responsibilities and attention they give to both parents.

The practice of having mothers bring children to medical appointments severely limits the impact a physician can have on the father-child relationship. Something as simple as asking fathers to bring children to appointments or asking parents to share this duty lets fathers know that they need to have regular contact with them to better understand their children. This can have a positive and lasting effect on the reduction of father hunger.

- Since **pediatricians** become involved with a family soon after the child is born, they can have a special role in fostering the parent-child relationship. Get each parent to discuss how their family life affected them and how they may want to be different as parents. Spend time talking about how hard it is for fathers to be involved directly in child care and give suggestions to guide them.

- At each new developmental stage (infancy, toddlerhood, pre-school, school-age, pre-teen, adolescence) **physicians** can give fathers suggestions about how their children's needs for father may change. Similarly, suggest how mothers can help fathers be involved.

- If parents express constant concern that their children may eat too much or too little, be too skinny or too fat, **physicians** should reassure them and advise that excessive parental interference may cause eating or weight problems. Also, they should see the child and parents more frequently to help monitor the situation. If either or both parents continue to be excessively worried, or to have a history of eating or weight problems themselves, a referral to a therapist who can help them with these problems is in order.

- **Physicians** also should further educate themselves about nutrition. They also should examine their own views about weight and be sure they are not contributing to dangerous dieting and body-image dissatisfaction in their young patients. A doctor's comment, such as, "You could stand to lose some weight," without direction and guidance about why, how, and what amount, can have disastrous effects on a youngster who is suffering from self-doubt or low self-esteem.

- **Physicians** should spend some time alone with their young patients to get to know them more directly and convey interest in them individually.

- **Physicians** should be sure to work with the other professionals involved to develop an approach if a youngster does have an eating or body-image problem. Coordinating efforts with the school and giving consistent messages will help parents address the problem. (See suggestions for "Schools and other systems" in Appendix A regarding how to approach and help families if an eating disorder is evident.)

- **Pediatricians** and **other family-care physicians** can help parents convey healthy attitudes about weight, eating, and body-image by paying attention to these issues early in a child's life. They should encourage both parents to:

  — set a positive example by trusting and accepting their own bodies

  — understand their attitudes toward weight and dieting

  — learn about the dangers of dieting

  — become sensitive to the constant messages from the dieting industry and the glorification of thinness by the fashion industry

  — talk to their children about the pressures they may feel to have the "perfect" body

  — discuss the changes adolescent bodies go through as they develop

— help their children to accept their bodies instead of constantly trying to change them

— praise their child's inner qualities and values and minimize
the importance of physical beauty

— help their child find constructive ways of expressing feelings so difficult emotions do not become converted into
bad eating habits

— let their children make mistakes and learn—be sure they
are not trying to make them perfect.

APPENDIX C

SUGGESTED STRATEGIES FOR THERAPISTS

Therapists play an important role in our attempts to improve the family structure. When clinicians do not understand their own father hunger, they are less able to address the issues related to men's role in the family and the distribution of power and responsibility between the sexes. However, if they have explored their family-of-origin experience, the balance between masculinity and femininity in their lives, and their attitudes toward women—particularly surrounding weight, food, body image, and sex-role functioning—they will be much more effective agents of change.

Although psychotherapy is always tricky, treating patients or families with eating problems is especially so. It is easy to develop rescue fantasies when the symptoms are so apparent and so potentially damaging, but therapists should be empowering the patient to face life. Developing simple explanations (similar to "if-only" reasoning or "it's just...)" is also tempting. For example, therapists sometimes blame the problems on one relationship, such as an absent dad or over-involved mom, instead of helping patients to understand why the family operated that way. Further-more, they may be oblivious to the dangerous psychological and physiological effects of eating disorders or to family issues, particularly the imbalance of roles and the function of the symptoms in the system. In essence, therapists may not appreciate how food, body image, weight, exercise, and appearance take on a special meaning in some families and how these can reflect a lack of connection between a dad and his daughter.

• **Therapists** need to explore the culture's impact on their experiences and attitudes and use this knowledge to guide their work with patients and families. This must include examining their expectations for men in families and their attitudes toward women, weight, food, appearance, and sex roles.

• **Therapists** need to educate themselves about the psychological and physiological consequences of eating disordered behaviors. They should help patients to understand these and to work toward symptom control so that the more long-term work of therapy can take place.

• **Therapists** must take time to explore and understand the patient's family dynamics and compare these to their own. With this information and an awareness of their own unresolved issues, therapists are more likely to change the pattern and avoid replicating the patient's past dynamics in the therapeutic relationship.

• **Therapists** must assess each case individually. The patient has the answers to her problems. The therapist's job is to listen acutely in order to guide patients to use their own wisdom. This can only occur when therapists understand the unique attributes of a patient and her family and resist the impulse to generalize.

• **Therapists** must encourage changes in families and in our culture that will allow a more equitable sharing of power and responsibility between the sexes so that fathers can be more involved in the family and daughters will feel accepted into the masculine world outside the family.

APPENDIX D

SUGGESTED STRATEGIES FOR OTHER PROFESSIONALS AND ADULTS

One obvious group that can help to improve father-child relationships is the legal profession. Attorneys, family relations specialists, legislators, judges, and courts should be careful to consider the importance of maintaining and enhancing this relationship in custody and divorce settlements. Professionals in these areas should let fathers know that their children need more than financial support, and that the conflicts between separated or divorced parents often result in fathers becoming more distant emotionally. They should let parents know about community resources that might assist them in effective parenting, especially any programs designed to help men be more active, constructive, and nurturing. Similarly, employers, industry, and government agencies can continue to develop family-oriented personnel policies that promote a more active role for fathers. Through a combination of personal efforts and attempts at programmatic change, we may accomplish something wonderful. These are only a few ideas. No matter what role you hold, you can do something about father hunger and its consequences.

- **Employee Assistance** or **Wellness Programs** can sponsor discussions about family relationships and men's and women's scripts to enhance the involvement of fathers and decrease the burdens on mothers.

- **Community organizations** could have family therapists and child development specialists teach men how to be more involved with their children, particularly during infancy and adolescence, when fathers are most apt to feel left out.

- **Libraries** could review books on parenting and on men's and women's social roles and work with the professions mentioned above to promote awareness and to improve men's role in families.

- **Employers, court personnel, legislators, government agencies,** and anyone else whose work can impact the family, should constantly examine their policies and methods to assess if they are helping or hurting the role of the father in the family. It is particularly important that we reconsider our public assistance programs, which are available to families only if father is absent. Efforts should be made, instead, to assist families to stay together and allow children a relationship with their fathers.

- **Attorneys, judges,** and **family relations court personnel** should encourage parents to mediate and resolve their differences and to consider the impact on children of a divorce, custody suit, or other disputes. They should speak specifically about the need children have for a relationship with both fathers and mothers, and urge them to find a way to handle their differences while still allowing children access to both parents.

- Ask your **local legislators** and **industry leaders** to promote policies that allow men to be more available to children. Flex-time and job-sharing do not have to be just for women. At the same time, you should be encouraging a fuller role in the workplace for women, so that girls can look forward to an adulthood where they will be valued, respected, and supported.

- **Adults** can do many simple things that will help children. When you watch television with them or read to them, ask them to share their perceptions. Find out what they thought about the story, how the people interacted, how fathers are portrayed, how the story ended, and how they would change it if they were writing it. This gives them the opportunity to find alternative approaches to problems, to communicate their thoughts, to feel your interest and attention, and to be active rather than passive participants in the world.

  In these situations you also can help children understand the power of our culture over all of us. Teach them to become critical consumers by informing them that images in the media do not always represent reality. Describe how advertisers manipulate us with their images and subliminal messages. Take advantage of any opportunity to convey that neither sex should be limited by stereotypes and outdated myths. Convey whenever and however you can that boys and girls, men and women, should live life to its fullest, connected to themselves and to others in satisfying relationships of respect, mutuality, and affection.

NOTES

CHAPTER 1

1. J. Piaget and B. Inhelder (1969). The Psychology of the Child. New York: Basic Books.

2. S. Minuchin, B.L. Rosman, and L. Baker (1978). Psychosomatic Families: Anorexia Nervosa in Context. Cambridge: Harvard Press.

3. M.S. Palazzoli (1978). Self–starvation: From individual to family therapy in the treatment of anorexia nervosa. New York: Jason Aronson.

4. M.S. Palazzoli (1988). The cybernetics of anorexia nervosa. In M. Selvini (ed.): The Work of Mara Selvini Palazzoli. Northvale, N.J.: Jason Aronson, p. 213–227. Quote can be found on p. 207.

5. K. Chernin (1985). The Hungry Self: Women, Eating and Identity. New York: Times Books.

CHAPTER 2

1. Random House American Dictionary and Family Reference Library, 1968, p 805.

2. Janeway, E. (1971). A Man's World, Woman's Place: A Study in Social Mythology. New York: Delta.

3. U.S. Bureau of Census (1984). Statistical Abstracts of the United States, p. 79.

4. Pittman F: The Secret Passions of Men. Lecture presented at the 47th Annual Conference of the American Association for Marriage and Family Therapy, Oct. 28, 1989, San Francisco, CA

5. Hetherington, E.M. (1973). Girls without fathers. Psychology Today, Feb., 47–52.

6. H.B. Biller (1976). The father and personality development: Paternal deprivation and sex-role development. In M.E. Lamb (ed.): The Role of the Father in Child Development. New York: John Wiley & Sons, p. 89–157.

CHAPTER 3

1. M.E. Lamb (1975). Fathers: Forgotten contributors to child development. Human Development, p 260.

2. Robert Bly, a mythopoet, is seen as the leader of the men's movement. See his book, R. Bly (1990). Iron John. New York: Addison Wesley.

3. For an examination of the father's role in female development, see C. Rivers, R. Barnett, G. Baruch (1979). Beyond Sugar and Spice: How Women Grow, Learn, and Thrive, NY: Ballatine Books.

4. This article is an excellent overview of the social and historical factors influencing men's parenting: J. Bloom–Feshback (1981), Historical perspectives on the father's role. In M.E. Lamb (ed.), The Role of the Father in Child Development. NY: John Wiley. (Quote can be found on p. 81.)

5. For a fascinating historical look at how women have been willing to change their appearance to express themselves and to feel accepted or acknowledged by others, see R. Freedman, (1989) Beauty Bound. New York: Harper & Row.

6. T. Berry Brazelton (1970). What makes a good father. Redbook, June.

7. Bloom–Feshback (1981), see note #4.

8. For a summary of the patterns in fathering and how these relate to historical influences in the United States, see M. Lamb (1986). The Father's Role: Applied Perspectives. NY: John Wiley.

9. For an account of how men's lives are affected by their relationships with their fathers, see S. Osherson (1986), Finding Our Fathers. New York: Fawcett Columbine.

10. S.H. Cath, A.R. Gurwitt, and J.M. Ross (1982). Father and Child: Developmental and Clinical Perspectives. Boston: Little, Brown, and Co., p. xxi.

11. J. Bowlby (1966). Maternal Care and Child Health. New York: Schoken Books, p. 13.

12. M. Greenberg and N. Norris (1974). Engrossment: The newborn's impact upon the father. American Journal of Orthopsychiatry 44, pp. 520–531.

13. C. McEnroe (1991). To Joey with love from a guy who grew to see fireballs. Hartford Courant, Sun., June 16, 1991, p. 1.

14. K. Pruett (1980). The nurturing male: A longitudinal study of primary nurturing fathers. In S.H. Cath, A. Gurwit and L. Gunsberg (eds.): Fathers and Their Families, Hillsdale, N.J.: The Analytic Press, pp. 389–409.

15. E.L. Abelin (1971). The role of the father in the separation/individu-

ation process. In J.B. McDevitt and C.F. Sethlage (eds.): Essays in Honor of Margaret Mahler. New York: International Universities Press, p. 229–252.

16. W.K. Redican (1976). Adult male-infant interactions in non–human primates. In M.E. Lamb (ed.) The Role of the Father in Child Development. New York: John Wiley.

17. M.W. West and M.S. Konner (1976). The role of the father: An anthropological perspective. In Lamb, see note #16.

18. M.E. Lamb and D. Oppenheim (1989). Fatherhood and father–child relationships: Five years of research. In S.H. Cath et al. (see #14), pp. 11–27.

19. K. Pruett, see note #14.

20. S. Orbach (1986). Hunger Strike: The Anorectic's Struggle as a Metaphor for our Age. New York: W.W. Norton, p. 42.

CHAPTER 4

1. C. Steiner-Adair (1989). Developing the voice of the wise woman: College students and bulimia. In L.C. Whitaker and W.N. Davis (eds.): The Bulimic College Student: Evaluation, Treatment, and Prevention. New York: Haworth Press, p. 152.

2. E.G. Belotti (1975). Little Girls. London: Writers and Readers Publishing Cooperative.

3. M. Jagger, K. Richards (1965). "I Can't Get No Satisfaction." ABKCO Records.

4. For elaboration on the notions of family loyalty and the potential long-term consequences for personal development and family functioning, see: I. Boszormenyi-Nagy, and G.M. Spark (1973). Invisible Loyalties. New York: Harper & Row.

5. R. Striegel-Moore, L.R. Silberstein, and J. Rodin (1986). Toward an understanding of risk factors for bulimia. American Psychologist 41 (3), 246–263.

6. C. Gilligan (1982). In a Different Voice: Psychological Theory and Women's Development. Cambridge: Harvard University Press, p. 100.

7. See: J. Lever (1976). Sex differences in the games children play. Social Problems 23, pp. 478–487.

See also: (1978). Sex differences in the complexity of children's play and games. American Sociological Review 43, 471–483.

8. R.S. George and M. Krondl (1983). Perceptions and food use of adolescent boys and girls. Nutrition and Behavior 1, 115–125

9. Greeting card by Cathy, from Recycled Paper Products, Universal Press Syndicate, Chicago, IL.

CHAPTER 5

1. J.B. Miller (1976). Toward a New Psychology of Women. Boston: Beacon Press, p. 83.

2. J. Bradshaw (1988). The Family. Deerfield Beach, Fl: Health Communications, Inc.

3. E.G. Belotti (1975). Little Girls. London: Writers and Readers Publishing Cooperative.

4. R. Striegel-Moore, L.R. Silberstein, and J. Rodin (1986). Toward an understanding of risk factors for bulimia. American Psychologist 41 (3), 246–263.

5. Gilligan's new work, Making Connections: The Relational Worlds of Adolescent Girls at Emma Willard School, is reviewed in an article by F. Prose, "Confident at 11, confused at 16," in the New York Times Magazine, Jan. 7, 1990; quote can be found on p. 23.

6. M. McGoldrick (1989). Women through the family life cycle. In M. McGoldrick, C.M. Anderson, F. Walsh (eds.): Women in Families. New York: Norton, pp. 200–227.

7. The Beauty Myth: How Images of Beauty Are Used Against Women, 1991, New York: William Morrow & Company, Naomi Wolf illustrates the tyranny of the quest for beauty and suggests that this may be the largest hurdle in women's struggle for equality.

8. See #4 above.

9. S. Orbach (1986). Hunger Strike. New York: Norton, p. 36.

10. S. MacLeod (1982). The Art of Starvation: A Story of Anorexia and Survival. New York: Schocken, p. 69.

11. P. Farb, G. Armelagos (1980). Consuming Passions: The Anthropology of Eating. New York: Washington Square Press.

12. R.C. Hawkins, S. Turell, and L.S. Jackson (1983). Desirable and undesirable masculine and feminine traits in relation to students' dietary tendencies and body image dissatisfaction. Sex Roles, 9, 705–724.

13. L. Mellin from the University of California at San Francisco testified on July 31, 1987 at a hearing in San Francisco held by the Congressional Select Committee on Children, Youth, and Families regarding her study of the frequency of dieting in children.

14. Testimony at Subcommittee on Regulation, Business Opportunities and Energy, U.S. House of Representatives Committee on Small Business, March 26, 1990.

15. Historical Tables: Budget of the United States Government: Fiscal Year 1992 (1991). Washington, D.C.: Executive Office of the President, Office of Management and Budget, p. 46.

16. Kim Chernin (1987). Reinventing Eve: Modern Woman in Search of Herself. New York: Harper & Row.

CHAPTER 6

1. G. Margolin and G. Patterson (1975). Differential consequences provided by mothers and fathers for their sons and daughters. Developmental Psychology 11, 537–538.

CHAPTER 7

1. C. Johnson and M. Connors (1987). The Etiology and Treatment of Bulimia Nervosa. New York: Basic Books.
2. M.P. Root, P. Fallon, and W.N. Friedrich (1986). Bulimia: A Systems Approach to Treatment. New York: Norton.
3. R. Oppenheimer, R. Howells, R.L. Palmer, D.A. Charloner (1985). Adverse sexual experience in childhood and clinical eating disorders: A preliminary description. Journal of Psychiatric Research, 19, 357–361.
4. K. Pruett (1987). The Nurturing Father: Journey Toward the Complete Man. New York: Warner.

CHAPTER 8

1. M. Levine (1987). How Schools Can Combat Eating Disorders. Washington, D.C.: National Education Association.
2. M.P. Root, P. Fallon, and W.N. Friedrich (1986). Bulimia: A Systems Approach to Treatment. New York: Norton.
3. W. Vandereycken, E. Kog, and J. Vanderlinden (1989). The Family Approach to Eating Disorders. New York, PMA Publishing Corp.
4. M.S. Palazzoli, see notes #3 & 4, chapter 1.
5. S. Minuchin et al., see note #2, chapter 1.
6. J.R. Kaplan (1980). A Woman's Conflict: The Special Relationship Between Women and Food. Englewood Cliffs, N.J.: Prentice–Hall, p.10.

CHAPTER 9

1. P. Caplan and I. Hall-McCorquodale (1985). Mother-blaming in major clinical journals. American Journal of Orthopsychiatry, 55 (3), 345–353.
2. Quote by Robert Bly, a poet and leader of mythopoetic men's movement. Cited by M. Miller (1988, July–Aug.). Tough Guys, Wounded hearts. Changes. p. 54.

3. R.S. Pasick, S. Gordon, and R.L. Meth (1990). Helping men understand themselves. In R.L. Meth and R.S. Pasick (eds.). Men in Therapy. New York: Guildford Press, pp. 152–180.

CHAPTER 10

1. J. Campbell (1972). Myths To Live By. New York: Bantam Books, p. 209.
2. S. Keen (1991). Fire in the Belly: On Being a Man. New York: Bantam Books. This great resource for men in search of new definitions of masculinity gives suggestions on how to form a "questing community" to help men address the pain and the potential of the male experience.
3. S. Osherson, p.18, (see note #9, chapter 3).
4. A. Napier (1988). The Fragile Bond. New York: Harper and Row. p. 84. Dr. Napier also gave an inspiring talk at the 47th Annual Conference of the American Association for Marriage and Family Therapy about our need to develop new heroes and to foster change in the family to support men as fathers. His talk, "Heroism, Men and Marriage" was part of a plenary session called, "Growing Up Married: Men and Commitment" and is available on audio tape from AAMFT, 1717 K Street, N.W., Suite 407, Washington, D.C. 20006
5. F. Pittman (1988). Bringing up father. The Family Therapy Networker, 12(3), p. 75.
6. G. Napier (1988), see note #4.
7. R.N. Atkins (1989). Divorce and Fathers: Some Intrapsychic Factors Affecting Outcome. In S.H. Cath, A. Gurwit, and L. Gunsberg (eds.), Fathers and their Families. Hillsdale, New Jersey: The Analytic Press, pp. 431-469.
8. F.F. Firstenberg, S.l. Peterson, C. Nord, N. Zill (1983). Life course of divorce: Marital disruption in parent contact. American Sociological Review, 38, 656-668.
9. P.L. Adams, J.R. Milner, N.A. Scherpf (1984). Fatherless Children. New York: J. Wiley and Sons.
10. W. Bennett and J. Gurin (1982). The Dieter's Dilemma. New York: Basic Books.
11. Weight Standards for Men and Women. Metropolitan Life Insurance Co. (1983).

CHAPTER 11

1. H. Goldhor-Lerner (1985). The Dance of Anger. New York: Harper & Row, p. 11.

2. H. Goldhor-Lerner, see note #1.

3. *ibid.*, p. 102.

4. D. McClelland (1965). Wanted: A new self-image for women. In R. J. Lifton (ed.), The Women in America. Boston: Houghton Mifflin Co., pp. 187-188.

5. M. Lamb and D. Oppenheim. See note #18, chapter 3.

6. C. Steiner-Adair. See note #1, chapter 4.

7. K. M. Pike and J. Rodin (1991). Mothers, Daughters, and Disordered Eating. Journal of Abnormal Psychology, 100(2), 198-204.

CHAPTER 12

1. Margery Williams (1975). The Velveteen Rabbit. New York: Avon Books, pp. 16-17.

CHAPTER 13

1. V. Phares and B. E. Compas (in press 1991). The role of fathers in child and adolescent psychopathology. Psychological Bulletin.

2. Attributed to Eldridge Cleaver. In John Bartlett, 1980, Familiar Quotations. Boston: Little, Brown, and Co., p. 913.

◆ ◆ ◆

INDEX

abandonment 54
absence-guilt 133
achievement orientation 53, 83
adolescence 23-4, 60, 77, 96; early maturation 98-100
advertising 68, 83
agricultural work 28
alienation 141-142
American tradition 26
anger 104-107, 138-139, 183-184
angerexia 139
anthropologists 39
behavior modification 81
Bowlby, John 36
Brazelton, Dr. T. Berry 31
Campbell, Joseph 178
cardiovascular disease 172-173
Chernin, Kim 11
children 4-6, 10-11, 20, 50, 118; development 22; influences 160
codependency 62

conflict avoidance 112-113
constricted communication 77-78, 113, 130-131
control 81-82, 107-109, 120
cooking and dieting 67-69
couvade 38
culture 4, 7-10, 16-18, 21, 23, 26, 40, 43, 52, 86, 124, 173; influences 12, 225; roles 4, 7, 17, 26, 39, 54, 86
de-selfing 182, 185
denial 21, 46, 113, 209
diet industry 69
divorce 159, 165-6, 195-196; divorce rate 37
extended family 221
families 3-12, 17-18, 25, 28, 47, 111-115, 120, 123-127, 163, 192, 201, 220-221; family dysfunction 25, 110-128; family life/ scripts 220; systems theory 7-10; family therapy 127, 156, 189, 222

fashion, adherance to 29-30
fashion industries 64-65
fathers: absent 37, 43, 44, 48, 95; coping with eating problems 174-176; expectant fathers 38; fathering 26, 36, 39, 41-42, 171-172, 176-178; father's role 8, 13-22, 26, 29-30, 36-37, 110, 149, 156, 224; listening 169-170; relationship with children 10, 24, 38-39, 41-42, 45, 53, 167, 218
female appearance, beauty, and identity 30, 63-67, 84, 192
femininity 18, 61, 22, 207
feminist movement 17, 26, 33-34, 56
food 53, 68, 120-122
Freud, Sigmund 36
Gilligan, Carol 59-60
Goldhor-Lerner, Harriet 183, 184
Great Depression 31
grief and loss 136-138, 140
guilt 61, 68, 116, 133-134, 187, 199
historical perspective 27-29
I-voice 185-186, 216-217
"if-only" 5-7, 11-12
incest 101, 108, 134
industrial revolution 19, 29-31

infant research 37
Konner, Melvin 39
labor, division of 27-28, 39, 131
Lamb, Michael 26
men's, attitudes toward women 160-162; beliefs about food, weight, and body-image 172-174; isolation 116; roles 4, 27, 191; as second-class citizens 26, 36
Metropolitan Life Insurance Company 173
Miller, Jean Baker 57
mother loss 44
mother's role 110, 117, 134
mother-bashing 134
mother/child relationship 5, 17, 36-37, 44, 187, 196-203
motherhood 30
multi-generational 4, 8, 9, 115, 123, 140
myths, traditions, and beliefs 7, 9, 13-16, 20-22, 48, 129-131, 171, 188, 192; about men 152-153,155-156, 226; about men's/women's roles 140-142
Napier, Gus 154
Orbach, Susie 40
Osherson, Sam 154
otheration 58, 61-62

Palazzoli, Mara Selvini 8-9
parenting 4, 20-21, 40, 43-44
parent's perspective 142-146
parent's relationship 37, 111-128
Pittman, Frank 22
pop-psychology 134
power 80, 111, 120, 223;
    redistributing power/roles 161-164, 190
puberty 65, 96, 98
becoming "real" 213, 214
Redican, William 39
self-esteem, self-worth 6, 11, 19, 35, 53, 121, 207, 222
sexuality 10, 23-24, 52, 95-97, 104; sex roles 28, 32, 34; sexual trauma 100-108; weight and sex appeal 174
social roles, etc.; see "culture"
subsistence societies 28
superwoman syndrome 191-192
therapy 106, 155-157, 170, 188-189, 201, 209-213
unintentional distancing 208
unrequited love 75-76
values, masculine 48-51
Velveteen Rabbit 213
Vietnam War 33-34
West, Mary 39
women's roles 23, 28, 32, 35, 59, 71, 191
World-War II 32